Passengers from Ireland

Lists of Passengers Arriving at American Ports Between 1811 and 1817

Transcribed from
The Shamrock or Hibernian Chronicle

By
DONALD M. SCHLEGEL

CLEAR~
FIELD

Reprinted for
Clearfield Company, Inc. by
Genealogical Publishing Co., Inc.
Baltimore, Maryland
1999

FOREWORD

In 1930 and 1931 alphabetized lists of about 5,150 passengers from Ireland were published in The Journal of the American Irish Historical Society. The lists covered the years 1811 and 1815-1816 and were compiled, respectively, by J. Dominick Hackett and Charles Montague Early. The source of their data was the New York newspaper The Shamrock or Hibernian Chronicle. The present work supersedes the Hackett and Early lists and includes all data on immigrants from the entire run of The Shamrock. Overall, publication of The Shamrock covered a seven-year period, with several gaps, as follows:

> December 15, 1810 - June 5, 1813
> June 18, 1814 - January 28, 1815
> September 2, 1815
> October 7, 1815 - August 3, 1816
> August 17, 1816
> December 2, 1816 - August 16, 1817

In addition to including passenger lists from periods not covered by the Hackett and Early lists, this work rectifies a few errors and omissions in those lists and presents all of the available detail concerning the passengers and their voyages. The lists are presented in their original format so that family groupings are apparent.

The Shamrock carried many death notices of Irish-Americans and, due to its wide circulation, carried many advertisements placed by persons seeking their relatives in other parts of the country. Abstracts of all of the death notices and advertisements which contain any reference to a person's place of origin in Ireland or date of immigration are grouped together following the passenger lists.

In copying the lists, the strong temptation to correct obvious typographical errors was avoided, so that correction or interpretation is left entirely to the user of the lists. In all, the names of 7,308 immigrants are included in this work.

INTRODUCTION

Irish Immigration to North America
in the Early Nineteenth Century

Irish immigration to the New World began, some believe, in the so-called Dark Ages, at the time of Brendan the Navigator, or even earlier. The first son of Erin whose presence in America is documented beyond any doubt was William of Galway, who sailed under Columbus on the Santa Maria. His story as "The first Irishman in America," by R. J. Kelly, was published in The Journal of the American Irish Historical Society, Vol. XXIX (1930-31), pp. 35-48.

Various studies of Irish immigration to North America in the eighteenth century have been published, but few complete records of immigration were kept. It is known that over 10,000 unemployed weavers left Ulster for North America in each of the years 1771 through 1774, probably marking the high-tide of Irish emigration in the eighteenth century.[1] Immigration was halted during the Revolution but was resumed after the peace was concluded in 1783. The Scotch-Irish and Irish of Ulster again made up the bulk of the immigrants, who numbered around 3,000 per year.[2]

No complete lists of immigrants were kept either in Ireland or in America in this period, but the port of Philadelphia did begin in 1798 to keep customs lists of cargo landed there, and these lists, from 1800, sometimes included the names of passengers. (From 1813 this was also true of New Orleans.) However, if a ship landed with no cargo, no list was filed, which was the case with most vessels carrying passengers from Ireland. For example, in the year 1800 some 3,000 Irish supposedly immigrated to the United States. Though the majority may have landed at New York, still a large number must have landed at Philadelphia. The Philadelphia customs lists, however, contain only three ships from Ireland and list the passengers on only two of these.

The British Passenger Vessel Act, which took effect in 1803, reduced the number of emigrants from Ireland by limiting the number of passengers which could be legally carried on a sailing vessel. Under this Act a vessel was restricted to one passenger for each two tons burden, after deducting equal amounts for the master and crew.

As a result of the Act, "By the laws of the British government as exercised in Ireland, and as respects persons wishing to emigrate from that country, it is required that such persons, previous to embarcation shall appear before some confidential officer of the British government in Ireland, to be by him examined, whether such person does not come under the prohibitory part of the law."[3] The surviving records indicate that the passengers often did not appear in person but that each ship's captain was required to submit to the government official a list of those wishing to embark on his vessel. Copies of these lists for the period March 29, 1803 through March 10, 1806 are contained in British

Museum additional manuscript No. 35932. Lists for the period through August 4, 1804 were published in Volumes LX, LXI, LXII, and LXVI of The New England Historical and Genealogical Register. In addition to the British Museum manuscript, the lists for the remainder of the three-year period are contained in Public Record Office of Northern Ireland transcript #521/1. The names of emigrants from the present six counties of Northern Ireland were indexed in the Report of the Deputy Keeper of the Records for the Year 1929. The names of the emigrants from the remainder of the island remain unpublished, but a copy of the lists can be obtained from the Public Record Office at cost.

The above-mentioned lists indicate an emigration of some 1100 persons per year. This rate probably continued until passage of the United States Embargo Act in December of 1807, which prohibited shipment of cargo from United States ports. Most of the Irish emigrants were carried in vessels which had carried freight to Ireland and were returning to the United States carrying only ballast. The Embargo Act, though never entirely effective, must have greatly reduced the number of vessels available for Irish emigration. Except for the short period from April to August of 1809, the Embargo Act and subsequent acts continued to limit commerce until May 1, 1810.[4]

The deteriorating economic position of the tenant farmers in Ireland, combined with the resumption of normal commerce, caused a new flood of emigration in 1811. Prices received by farmers for their crops in 1811 were only one half or less of their prices in the previous year. These low prices were paid to the farmers in bank notes, the only circulating currency. The farmers were required to exchange the bank notes for gold guineas, which were demanded for the rent payments by the landlords' agents. Guineas were so scarce that the farmers had to pay a premium of four shillings over face value for each of the golden coins. "Nay, it is further stated, that the agents employ persons to sell the gold to the tenantry, and that the same guineas are often sold by those wretches 10 times in one day."[5] A fifty percent increase in taxes, combined with the scarcity of gold, brought business to a standstill and brought many to bankruptcy.[6]

One other factor contributing to the emigration at this time was the expiration of many old leases and the doubling, trebling, and even quadrupling of rents demanded for their renewal. "Many who under their old leases made comfortable livings and laid up a little from year to year, foresaw that under the new leases they would neither be able to make anything nor to keep what they made. They therefore wisely concluded to leave a country which was continually sinking deeper in debt, distress, and despair..." At rates of from eight to twelve guineas per adult passenger, only the better class of tenant farmers could afford to leave the country. The poor remained, except for those Catholics who, driven to desperation by persecutions, fled to Scotland.[7]

As conditions in England deteriorated also, many reportedly starving factory laborers made their way to Ireland and there took ship for the United States. Many of the passengers who arrived in 1812 therefore might have resided in Ireland for only a few days.[8]

On their arrival in the United States, the Irish immigrants of this period found a weekly newspaper devoted exclusively to their own interests. The Shamrock or Hibernian Chronicle was founded in New York City by Edward Gillespy and was first published on December 15, 1810. News from Ireland, news of Irish in America, and other items of interest to the immigrants were published in this newspaper. Distribution, via the postal system, was made to annual subscribers who were enrolled by agents in most of the nation's major cities and towns. It is thanks to this newspaper that the names and former residences of many of the Irish immigrants of this period have been preserved. The very first issue stated that "The Marine List shall consist of Vessels in the Irish Trade - The Names of Passengers arriving in any of the ports of this country, shall be carefully collected and given, which must prove extremely satisfactory to their friends resident here, and facillitate their communication with each other." This effort no doubt has also proved "extremely satisfactory" to the distant descendants of the immigrants.

The lists were difficult to obtain. Official customs lists were used when available; in some cases, the names were obtained from one of the passengers. Once, the names of passengers who signed a published commendation of their ship's captain was the only list the editor could locate. All too often, no list could be obtained, despite efforts that "none shall intentionally be omitted."[9]

The lists of passengers and vessels published in The Shamrock in 1811, which did not include all vessels arriving in the United States from Ireland, mention over 3800 passengers. This verifies editorial remarks that immigration was unusually heavy that year.[10]

Both the British Museum lists and the lists in The Shamrock indicate that each year's sailing season began around March, peaked in May and June, and then declined, with the last vessels departing late in the autumn. Crossings as short as twenty-nine days were made in good weather, but those ships leaving Ireland in the autumn were likely to be struck by North Atlantic storms and gales, with crossings as long as seventy-one days recorded.

Besides the normal dangers of seafaring, emigrants of 1811 and 1812 faced the twin threats of impressment aboard British war vessels and of a forced change of destination to British Canadian provinces. These threats were based on long-standing British policy. In the first case, England had no military conscription to supply its army; however, the naval force was maintained largely by impressment, the process of forcing or pressing able-bodied men into the service. This policy was freely applied to the emigrants from Ireland, because England, and all European nations, were still clinging to the eighteenth-century doctrine of indefeasible allegiance: once a Frenchman, always a Frenchman; once an Englishman, always an Englishman.[11] In the second case, despite loud protests to the contrary, British naval officers used the technicality of passengers supposedly not properly clearing the Irish customs-house to send whole shiploads of passengers to St. John's in Nova Scotia. It was implied by some that the government policy was dictated in part by the need for laborers on Lord Townshend's estate on that island.[12]

Families were mercilessly divided in order that the strength of the British navy and the profitability of the St. John's settlement could be maintained.

The general concensus that open warfare between the United States and Great Britain was fast approaching did nothing to abate the desire of the Irish to emigrate in 1812.[13] It did contribute to the rate of impressment of emigrants into the British navy, for, as one officer put it, he saw no point in allowing able-bodied men to proceed to that Republican country which he would soon be fighting against. War was declared on June 19, 1812, but those vessels already at sea continued on their way for American ports. By the time the schooner Eunice glided into New York harbor in September, the immigration of over 1,720 Irish men, women, and children had been noted in The Shamrock since the first of the year.

American vessels trapped in Irish ports at the declaration of war were immediately taken by the British. Near Londonderry, His Majesty's schooner Barbara, under one Lieutenant Morgan, after pressing a group of Irish fishermen, proceeded to Moville Bay where four American vessels were making arrangements to put to sea. The American crewmen and many of the passengers were seized and very roughly treated. The vessels involved were the ship Bristol, under Captain Barker, the Mary, and two others. The people of Londonderry were appalled at this treatment of their trading partners and of their neighbors and countrymen.[14]

Even during the War of 1812 the flow of Irish emigrants was not completely halted. The cartel ships which carried official communications between the warring governments and performed other legal business were allowed to carry a limited number of passengers. One list of such passengers arriving in May of 1813 was published in The Shamrock.[15] In addition to these legal emigrants, if published newspaper reports are to be believed, the permanent passage of many Irishmen to America was unwittingly effected by the British government itself. A letter dated Albany, New York, October 4, 1814 and published on October 8 states:

> In your last Shamrock I perceived an article on the subject of the desertion of Irishmen from the ranks of the enemy, and their desire to enlist at home, in order that they might on landing on our shores embrace the first opportunity of joining the sons of liberty. Of the friendly disposition of Irishmen in general to our government and country, I entertain no doubt, but be assured, that desertion from the British army is by no means confined to Irishmen; the streets of Albany are at present literally crowded with deserters, who are chiefly Germans, with a few Italians, French, and Irish, who came over during the battle of Plattsburg. I yesterday conversed with a young man from the North of Ireland, who assured me, that upwards of 600 men came over on that occasion, besides a constant daily desertion of 10 to 30 men previous to that affair.

A profitable search for immigrants' names might someday be made in the records of the British army.

The treaty of peace was agreed upon December 24, 1814 and was ratified on February 11, 1815. The first American vessel arrived at Belfast on April 6 carrying flaxseed, ashes, and other goods. According to the Ulster Recorder of Belfast:

> The heartfelt joy which beamed on every countenance throughout our streets, on learning this first arrival of their old American friends, can be easily conceived by those who will consider that the dearest and most affectionate connexions which bind humanity together, exist between the people of the North of Ireland, and the independent and victorious people of America. There is scarcely a cabin in our province, which cannot claim a relative in the land of civil and religious freedom. ...
> In Liverpool, the American vessels were received with the cheerings of thousands - is Belfast less alive to the sentiment of freedom, than the old advocates of the Slave Trade? Belfast should illuminate - our houses should be the pictures of our hearts. The people should, in this instance, exercise their high pre-rogative, and a general illumination either to-night or to-morrow should be insisted upon![16]

Unfortunately, The Shamrock halted publication after its edition of January 28, 1815, and did not resume until September 2. Therefore the names of the first passengers to arrive in New York after the resumption of normal commerce have not been preserved.

Weather for the harvest season of 1815 in Ireland held good through mid-November, and a good harvest was gathered in. However, since the peace had been declared, food prices were depressed while taxes and rents remained high.[17] The Shamrock mentioned over 855 passengers in the period from September 1 through December 4.

Economic conditions in Ireland in 1816 again caused a heavy flow of emigration. Tenants were still subject to high taxes to pay for the late war. Many landlords and agents were holding the tenants to the terms of leases signed during the war, when high prices paid for farm produce had pushed rents high. With the coming of peace, the value of produce fell drastically, leaving the tenants without the means to meet the landlords' demands. The problem spread to a higher class than had been affected previously, as testified by a letter from Naas in County Kildare:

> Hitherto emigration from this part of the island was nearly confined to the poorest order of the inhabitants; it now includes the more wealthy class, that is snug farmers, who were accustomed to live comfortable and afford their families to appear and rank as gentlemen. These are the persons who, foreseeing that a few years must reduce them to poverty, are providing against the misfortune, by a timely removal of themselves, their families and their fortunes, to the new world. The usual wish to emigrate continues and increases among the labouring class; and the last shilling of the price of the last cow, frequently goes to effect the favourite object.[18]

The Shamrock mentions 2320 passengers from Ireland during the period between January 1 and August 16, 1816 (when publication halted again for several months). This represents only a fraction of the actual immigration. Figures published in Niles' Weekly Register (XIII, 35) indicate that a total of about 800 Irish immigrants landed in the period from July 18 through August 15, while The Shamrock mentions only 455 passengers in the same period.

The majority of the Irish immigrants of 1816 landed at New York. Those who remained in that city found little employment available and became discouraged when their meagre resources were exhausted. Some re-embarked for Ireland. Others were enticed by British agents to accept a free passage to Canada, only to find conditions there even more discouraging than in New York. Some who remained in the city were aided by the Shamrock Friendly Association, which matched the unemployed immigrants with available jobs. Those who found the happiest solution to the problem were those who travelled inland to the eastern farming regions, where work and homes were found, or travelled beyond to the new states and territories west of the Appalachians. Residents of Zanesville reported that forty to fifty wagons of western migrants crossed the Muskingum River there each day. Early statehood was expected for Missouri and Illinois because of the flood of "native" Americans and entire immigrant families.[19]

A harvest failure in Ireland caused by six weeks of rain, combined with continued high taxes and the other perennial problems of the Irish, caused emigration to continue at an increased rate in 1817.[20] Some 13,000 Irishmen arrived on the shores of the United States that year,[21] although The Shamrock mentions only about 935 between January 1 and August 13, 1817. The Shamrock ceased publication after its issue of August 16, 1817.

Emigration from Ireland increased in each succeeding year, but until January of 1820, when the Federal government began keeping records, the names of the immigrants are unrecorded, except for those in the Philadelphia and New Orleans cargo lists.

[1] Beckett, James C., The Making of Modern Ireland, 1603-1923 (New York: Knopf, 1966), p. 206. Also Constantine Fitzgibbon, Red Hand: The Ulster Colony (Garden City: Doubleday, 1972).

[2] New Catholic Encyclopedia (New York: McGraw-Hill, 1967), Vol. VII, p. 645.

[3] The Shamrock, July 13, 1811.

[4] Channing, Edward, The Jeffersonian System, 1801-1811; Vol. XII of The American Nation: A History (New York & London: Harper & Brothers, 1906), pp. 213, 228, 236, 245, 249.

[5] The Shamrock, June 22, 1811.

[6] Ibid., June 29, 1811.

[7] Ibid., June 29, 1811, Nov. 16, 1811, Nov. 23, 1811, Oct. 14, 1815, Dec. 16, 1815.

[8] Ibid., May 9, 1812.

[9] Ibid., June 15, 1811.

[10] Ibid., Nov. 16, 1811.

[11] Channing, op. cit., pp. 170, 172.

[12] The Shamrock, Aug. 10, 1811, June 13, 1812.

[13] Ibid., July 11, 1812.

[14] Ibid., July 11, 1812.

[15] Ibid., May 29, 1813.

[16] Ibid., Oct. 21, 1815.

[17] Ibid., Nov. 25, 1815, Dec. 2, 1815.

[18] Ibid., April 20, 1816, July 20, 1816.

[19] Ibid., Dec. 2, 1816, Dec. 7, 1816, Dec. 14, 1816.

[20] Ibid., Feb. 8, 1817, May 17, 1817.

[21] North American Review, XL, 460n.

Summary of Vessels

The summary beginning on the page opposite includes all vessels from Ireland mentioned in The Shamrock, not just those for which passenger lists were printed. Under the column headed "Passengers" the word "list" indicates that a list was published; a number in parentheses indicates the minimum number of passengers indicated by the information contained in the list; a plain number indicates a number of passengers specifically stated in The Shamrock; "yes" indicates the presence of an unspecified number of passengers; "commendation" or "advertisement" indicates passenger names taken from a paid article to which their names were appended; and "--" indicates a vessel from Ireland for which no indication was given as to the presence of passengers.

The vessels are numbered in order of their arrival in the United States for each year. For example, the Golconda is number 11-16, the sixteenth arrival noted in The Shamrock during the year 1811.

er	Name of Vessel	Departed	Arrived	Passengers
1	Ship Erin	Dublin	New York	list (64)
1	Brig Harvey Hide	Belfast	New York	list (64)
2	Brig Hannibal	Belfast	Amboy	list (43)
3	Brig Perseverance	Belfast	New York	list (40)
4	Ship Protection	Belfast	Amboy	list (79)
5	Ship Radius	Cork	New York	list (63)
6	Algernon	Belfast	New York	list (148)
7	Westpoint	Londonderry	New York	105, list
8	Jupiter	Belfast	New York	list (97)
9	Brig Orlando	Belfast	New York	55, list
10	Mary Augusta	Newry	New York	102
11	Ship Aeolus	Newry	New York	80, list
12	Ship Erin	Dublin	New York	--
13	Ship John Watson	Dublin	New York	--
14	Ship Africa	Belfast	New York	list (105)
15	Ship Alexandria	Londonderry	New York	85, list
16	Golconda	Londonderry	New York	list (84)
17	Brig Patty	Newry	Philadelphia	list (12)
18	Ship Mary	Londonderry	Philadelphia	list (97)
19	Ship Shamrock	Dublin	New York	60, list
20	Ship Huntress	Dublin	New York	47, list
21	Ship Hibernia	Belfast	New York	100, list
22	Washington	Londonderry	New York	119
23	Friendship	Kinsale	New York	--
24	Belisarius	Dublin	New York	list (73)
25	Ship Joseph and Phoebe	Londonderry	Baltimore	list (102)
26	Ship Rising States	Newry	Philadelphia	list (33)
27	President	Newry	New York	92
28	Massachusetts	Dublin	New York	--
29	Brig Isaac	Cork	Philadelphia	list (4)
30	Ship Medford	Newry	Philadelphia	yes
31	Brig Juno	Belfast	New York	100, list
32	Ship Mexicana	Dublin	Amboy	100
33	Brig Hespa	Newry	New York	62
34	Ship Ariade	Belfast	New York	114
35	Ship Ann	Londonderry	New York	36, list
36	Ship Jefferson	Londonderry	Amboy	yes
37	Ship Prosperity	Londonderry	Philadelphia	130
38	Ship Fame	Londonderry	Philadelphia	list (52)
39	Ship Boyne	Lough Swilly	Philadelphia	yes
40	Ship Maria Duplex	Belfast	New York	list (15)
41	Iris	Newry	Amboy	yes
42	Ship Protection	Belfast	New York	list (71)
43	White Oak	Dublin	New York	list (23)
44	Ship Mariner	Londonderry	New London	list (65)
45	Ship Caroline	Lough Swilly	New York	58
46	Ship Fanny and Almira	Belfast	New York	30
47	Ship Favourite	Dublin (Cork)	New York	56
48	Ship Gleaner	Londonderry	Philadelphia	112
49	Brig Orlando	Belfast	Barnstable	yes
50	Keziah	Belfast	New London	yes
51	Ship Harmony	Londonderry	Philadelphia	list (104)
52	Brig Swift	Dublin	New York	yes
53	Ship Radius	Londonderry	New York	yes; commendation

11-54	Ship Erin	Dublin	New York	list (10)
11-55	Ship Westpoint	Londonderry	New York	list (81)
11-56	Ship Hibernia	Belfast	New York	list (45)
11-57	Ship Rover	Dublin	New York	--
11-58	Ship Aeolus	Newry	New York	list (57)
11-59	Ship Alexander	Londonderry	New York	list (37)
11-60	Alknomac	Sligo	Newport	79, list
11-61	Ship Columbia	Belfast	New York	yes
11-62	Ship Raleigh	Dublin	New York	list (10)
12-1	Ship Joseph and Phoebe	Londonderry	Hempstead	list (32)
12-2	Brig Eliza	Sligo	Philadelphia	list (39)
12-3	Ship Erin	Dublin	New York	list (35)
12-4	Ship Support	Dublin	New York	list (25)
12-5	Ship Protection	Belfast	New York	list (49)
12-6	Ship Favourite	Dublin	New York	list (16)
12-7	Ship Hibernia	Belfast	New York	93, list
12-8	Ship Mary Augusta	Londonderry	New York	67, list
12-9	Ship Triton	Belfast	New York	90
12-10	Ship Westpoint	Londonderry	New York	list (104)
12-11	Ship Radius	Londonderry	New York	100, list
12-12	Ship Maria Duplex	Dublin	New York	6, list
12-13	Ship Eliza	Londonderry	Philadelphia	list (90)
12-14	Ship Massasoit	Newry	New York	list (67)
12-15	Bark Edward	Newry	New York	list (58)
12-16	Ship Margaret	Dublin	New York	yes
12-17	Brig Hespa	Londonderry	New York	list (76)
12-18	Brig Mary	Coleraine	New York	list (48)
12-19	Ship Alexander	Londonderry	New York	list (115)
12-20	Augusta	Londonderry	New York	--
12-21	Aeolus	Newry	New York	--
12-22	Perseverance	Dublin	New York	--
12-23	Standard	Newry	New York	--
12-24	Enterprise	Newry	New York	--
12-25	Susannah	Londonderry	New York	--
12-26	Brig Pleiades	Belfast	New York	yes
12-27	Ship Rising States	Newry	Philadelphia	list (68)
12-28	Brig Retrieve	Londonderry	Philadelphia	list (82)
12-29	Brig Pallas	Lough Swilly	Philadelphia	list (56)
12-30	Ship Mary	Londonderry	Philadelphia	list (97)
12-31	Ship Bristol	Londonderry	New York	list (54)
12-32	Ship Venus	Londonderry	New York	list (61)
12-33	Ship Atlas	Belfast	New York	list (39)
12-34	Felix	Galway	New York	list (26)
12-35	Ship Ontario	Newry	New York	yes
12-36	Ship North Star	Londonderry	Bath	yes
12-37	Ship Bellisarius	Belfast	----	52
12-38	Brig Prudence	Dublin	Halifax	yes
12-39	Brig Narind	Newry	New York	list (47)
12-40	Schooner Eunice	Londonderry	New York	list (27)
13-1	Brig Catherine Ray	Liverpool	New York	list (20)
15-1	Brig Nautilus	Dublin	New York	list (18)
15-2	Ship Amphion	Dublin	New York	list (48)
15-3	Brig Helen	Sligo	New York	list (38)
15-4	Ship Virginia	Waterford	New York	list (33)

5-5	Brig Christopher	Belfast	New York	list (37)
5-6	Schooner Mary	Dublin	New York	list (23)
5-7	Brig Mary	Dublin	Newport	77
5-8	Ship George	Belfast	New York	list (54)
5-9	Ship James Bailey	Belfast	New York	list (98)
5-10	Ship George and Albert	Dublin	Philadelphia	list (43)
5-11	Brig Maria	Dublin	New York	list (2)
5-12	Brig Charles	Dublin	New York	list (23)
5-13	Brig Two Friends	Halifax	New York	list (2)
5-14	Ship William	Liverpool	New York	list (2)
5-15	Ship Mexico	Liverpool	New York	list (4)
5-16	Ship Marcus Hill	Londonderry	New York	list (121)
5-17	Brig Orient	Dublin	New York	list (35)
5-18	Ship Westpoint	Belfast	New York	list (45)
5-19	Ship Sally	Dublin	New York	list (57)
5-20	Ship Minerva	Liverpool	New York	list (4)
5-21	Barque Courier	Lisbon	New York	list (4)
5-22	Brig Favorite	Demerara	New York	list (1)
5-23	Ship Emperor Alexander	Londonderry	New York	list (64)
5-24	Ship Leda	Newry	Long Island	advertisement, 60
6-1	Brig Shannon	Belfast	New York	list (33)
6-2	Ship Ontario	Dublin	New York	list (55)
6-3	Ship Amphion	Dublin	New York	list (20)
6-4	Ship Erin	Dublin	New York	list (31)
6-5	Ship Dublin Packet	Dublin	New York	list (39)
6-6	Ship Anne	Cork	New York	list (32)
6-7	Brig Hannah	Dublin	New York	list (1)
6-8	Ship Lorenzo	Belfast	New York	list (53)
6-9	Brig Nancy	Newry	Philadelphia	list (22)
6-10	Ship Globe	Newry	Baltimore	list (23)
6-11	Brig Elizabeth	Belfast	New York	list (46)
6-12	Ship Dido	Newry	Philadelphia	list (22)
6-13	Brig John	Belfast	New York	list (18)
6-14	Brig Charles Fawcett	Dublin	New York	list (31)
6-15	Brig Hare	Galway	New York	list (29)
16-16	Ship Active	Londonderry	Philadelphia	list (25)
16-17	Ship Louisa	Dublin	Philadelphia	list (26)
16-18	Ship Aeolus	Newry	New York	list (36)
16-19	Brig London	Newry	New York	list (24)
16-20	Brig Wilson	Dublin	New York	list (38)
16-21	Ship Conistoga	Dublin	Philadelphia	list (45)
16-22	Ship Foster	Londonderry	New York	list (50)
16-23	Ship Westpoint	Belfast	New York	list (45)
16-24	Ship Enterprise	Londonderry	New York	list (33)
16-25	Brig Falcon	Londonderry	New York	list (34)
16-26	Ship Jane	Londonderry	Philadelphia	list (33)
16-27	Schooner William	Belfast	New York	list (20)
16-28	Ship Marcus Hill	Londonderry	New York	list (155)
16-29	Ship Niagra	Londonderry	New York	list (34)
16-30	Brig Ossian	Belfast	New York	list (90)
16-31	Ship George	Belfast	Philadelphia	list (46)
16-32	Brig Sophia	Belfast	New York	List (82)
16-33	Brig Foundling	Sligo	New York	list (90)
16-34	Brig Orient	Sligo	New York	list (56)
16-35	Ship Bristol	Dublin	New York	list (47)

16-36	Brig Ceres	Dublin	Philadelphia	list	(37)
16-37	Ship Dibby and Eliza	Dublin	New York	list	(65)
16-38	Packet Montague	----	New York	list	(2)
16-39	Brig Only Son	Dublin	Philadelphia	list	(29)
16-40	Brig George	Belfast	New York	list	(90)
16-41	Brig Actress	Dublin	New London	list	(32)
16-42	Ship Prince of Brazil	Belfast	New York	list	(98)
16-43	Ship Samuel	Newry	New York	--	
16-44	Ship Neptune	Newry	New York	--	
16-45	Ship Alpha	Belfast	Philadélphia	list	(46)
16-46	Brig Boudain	Newry	New York	list	(37)
16-47	Brig John	Galway	New York	list	(40)
16-48	Ship Ontario	Dublin	New York	list	(96)
16-49	Brig Margaret	Sligo	New York	list	(52)
16-50	Brig Mount-Bay	Londonderry	New York	list	(127)
16-51	Brig Barkley	Londonderry	New York	list	(57)
16-52	Brig Juno	Sligo	New London	list	(33)
16-53	Ship Bristol	Dublin	New York	list	(40)
17-1	Ship Neptune	Belfast	New York	list	(32)
17-2	Ship Rose in Bloom	Belfast	New York	list	(30)
17-3	Ship Anne Alexander	Dublin	New York	list	(11)
17-4	Brig Calypso	Dublin	New York	list	(13)
17-5	Ship Columbus	Liverpool	New York	list	(1)
17-6	Ship Loyal Sam	Sligo	New York	list	(12)
17-7	Ship Dublin Packet	Dublin	New York	list	(37)
17-8	Brig Anne	Dublin	New York	list	(30)
17-9	Brig Ann	Belfast	New York	list	(25)
17-10	Ship Ontario	Dublin	New York	list	(51)
17-11	Ship Neptune	Dublin	New York	list	(32)
17-12	Brig Frances	Sligo	New York	list	(2)
17-13	Ship Commodore Perry	Sligo	New York	list	(51)
17-14	Ship Westpoint	Belfast	New York	list	(48)
17-15	Ship Hibernia	Londonderry	New York	list	(50)
17-16	Ship Anne	Cork	New York	list	(17)
17-17	Brig Hugh Wallace	Belfast	Norfolk	list	(47)
17-18	Brig Tiffin	Dublin	New York	list	(22)
17-19	Ship Victory	Limerick	New Bedford	list	(29)
17-20	Ship Aeolus	Londonderry	New York	list	(38)
17-21	Brig Factor	Newry	New York	list	(48)
17-22	Ship Foster	Belfast	New York	list	(57)
17-23	Ship Down	Belfast	New York	list	(59)
17-24	Ship Bristol	Newry	New York	list	(43)
17-25	Schooner Vigilant	Belfast	New York	list	(3)
17-26	Brig Britannia	Newry	New York	list	(26)
17-27	Ship Calpe	Dublin	New York	list	(30)
17-28	Brig Agnes	Waterford	New York	list	(48)
17-29	Ship Erin	Dublin	New York	list	(43)

10-1

(a) Ship <u>Erin</u>, Captain Murphy, from Dublin, arrived at New York before
December 29, 1810.

(b) On board the ship <u>Erin</u>, 3 weeks previous to her arrival at this port,
died Mr. Patrick Walsh, aged 22, son to Mr. John Walsh, gardner, of New
York city.

(c)

Miss W. Larkin	Co. Wexford	John Bishop	
Miss F. Walsh	"	and wife	Co. Dublin
John Barry	Co. Louth	Patrick M'Cabe	"
Edward Furlong	Co. Wexford	James O'Brien	Co. Meath
Michael Butler	"	Terrence Farley	Co. Cavan
Mary Butler	"	Isabella Plaus	Co. Longford
Bridget Rigan	"	Joseph Manly	New York
Bridget Byrnes	Co. Louth	Emanuel Toole	Dublin
John Byrnes	"	William Bleakly	"
Nicholas Byrnes	"	John Fitzgerald	"
C. Byrnes, junr.	"	John Roberts	"
Francis Duffy	Co. Monaghan	Darby Kelly	Co. Meath
Fargus Duffy	"	Mathew Neall	
Mary Walsh	Co. Galway	and wife	Co. Meath
John Walsh (child)	"	Edw. M'Guinness	"
William Ray	Co. Cavan	Patrick Keally	Dublin
Mrs. H. Bowles	Co. Sligo	John Thomas	Ballyhayes
James M'Mally	Co. Meath	Thomas Hales	Glasstown
Patrick Ryan	Co. Wexford	Francis Leonard	"
William Malvin,		James West	"
wife, 5 sons, &		John M'Brien	"
4 daughters	Co. Cavan	Simon Horan	Mullicath
Owen Duffy	Co. Monaghan	Thomas Hearn	New York
Ann Weapher	Rathfarnham	J. Cunningham	Sligo
James Murphy	Co. Louth	Christian Wogan	Co. Dublin
John Giles	Baillboro	James Duffy	Co. Cavan
Andrew Waters	Co. Wexford	Wm. Floughsby	Dublin
William Stewart	Belfast	Mary Ryan	New Ross, Co. Wexford

THE AVAILABLE INFORMATION CONCERNING EACH VESSEL
HAS BEEN DIVIDED INTO THE FOLLOWING THREE SECTIONS:

(a) Name of vessel, name of captain, length of journey and port of departure,
port and date of arrival, number of passengers.

(b) Other news or comments concerning the vessel, its journey, or its
passengers.

(c) Passenger list.

(a) Brig <u>Harvey Hide</u>, Captain Thomas Parker, 77 days from Belfast via Newport, arrived at New York before January 5, 1811.

(b) Commendation of Captain Parker signed by:

Thomas Rynoldson	James Montgomery
Thomas Gilliton	Robert Raney
Dennis M'Curdy	James M'Lance
Isaac Johnson	William Davis
James Hall	James Moore

(c) Name, parish, county of residence:

William Simpson, Lochgall, Armagh	H. Mubrea, Newtonards, Down
Mrs. John Speirs, Doneghore, Antrim	James Moore, Donaghmore, Tyrone
William Davis, Blairis, Down	John Brown, Lochgall, Antrim
Robert Harvey, " "	Francis Brown, Kelbroghts, Antrim
Mrs. R. Harvey, " "	David Bell, Lochgall, Armagh
Leonard Dobbin, Killeman, Down	John Davidson, " "
Isaac Jenkinson, Lochgall, Armagh	Mrs. W. Campbell, Blairis, Down
Mrs. Jenkinson " "	Wm. Frances, Drumall, Antrim
James Jenkinson " "	Martha Frances, " "
Elizabeth Jenkinson " "	James Auld, Grange, Antrim
Isaac Jenkinson " "	Mury Auld, " "
Ann Jenkinson " "	Robert Grendle, Kellmore, Armagh
Mrs. Wm. Miller, Ahahill, Antrim	Sarah Grendle, " "
William Davis, Hillsboro, Down	William Coil, Daryluren, Tyrone
James Coal, Drumboa, Down	Peter Coil, " "
Alley Coal, " "	Sarah Coil, " "
J. Montgomery, Counmoney, Antrim	Rosa Coil, " "
Mrs. J. Kennedy, Douaghmore, Tyrone	John M'Lanna, " "
William Law, Kalmchie, Down	Thomas Lietson, Lurne, Antrim
John Aslein, Belfast, Antrim	Mary Lietson, " "
James Couples, Aughderg, Down	Mary Harrison, Aughdary, Down
Elizabeth Couples, " "	John Harrison, " "
Alex M'Murray, Kelmore, Armagh	John Liston, Kellmore, Armagh
Hannah M'Murray, Kelmore, Armagh	Eliza Liston, " "
James Spiers, Donegoare, Antrim	T. Anderson, Newtonards, Down
James M'Cance, Newtonards, Down	George Anderson, " "
Samuel Anderson, " "	Jennet Anderson, " "
John Welsh, " "	Alex. M'Kenzie, Lochgall, Armagh
Louisa Welsh, " "	Philip M'Kenzie, " "
John M'Kenzie, " "	Ralph M'Kenzie, " "

11-2

(a) Brig Hannibal, departed Belfast on January 2, landed at Amboy before March 23, 1811.

(b) "We are highly gratified to see many fine healthy young men by the above vessel..."
The list of passengers was not a customs list, but was "furnished us by one of themselves."

(c)

Mapshall Fendlay	Lisburn	John Drain	Co. Antrim
Joseph Knox	Balleybur	John M'Fall	Portglenone
Peter Hughes	"	Owen M'Peak	"
Robert M'Elwrath,		Jas. Hughes	Dublin
wife and child	Hollowood	James Connor	Lesburn
Nathaniel Alsop		Patrick Garvin	"
and wife	Seafield	Charles Davis	Armagh
Geo. Brown, wife		Charles Ferris	"
and 7 children	Banbridge	Patrick Mollin,	
John Carr	Hillsboro	wife & 4 children	"
Henry Cochrane	Co. Mayo	Robert English	Scotland
William Cochrane	"	Wm. Ross, wife	
Robert Cochrane	"	and 4 children	Vernersbridge
Henry Drain	Co. Antrim		

11-3

(a) Brig Perseverance, Captain George B. Crawford, 57 days from Belfast, landed at New York on March 27, 1811.

(b) Commendation of Captain Crawford signed by:

S. Stewart		Wm. Danwoody
Wm. Donnelly	Cabin	John Danwoody
Henry Scott	passengers	Elizabeth Thompson
Thomas Donalson		David Park
Robert Thompson		Moses Montgomery

Among the passengers were "10 weavers, 1 miller, 1 bricklayer, 1 saddler, 1 hosler, 1 cooper, and 1 gardner. N.B. Three of the first are Cotton Weavers."

(c)

Andrew Stewart, wife		William Donnelly	Belfast
and one child	Stewartstown	Robert Thompson	
George Wallace	Town of Antrim	and wife	"
Hugh M'Mullan	Co. Down	John Dauwoody	"
Moses Montgomery,		Wm. Danwoody	"
wife and three		David Park	"
children	Killele	Matthew M'Murrey	"
Alexander White	Dromore	William Stewart	Dunsmurry
James Nielson	"	Alexan. Stewart	"
Eliza'h Nielson		Jane Stewart Senr.	"
and one child	"	Jane Stewart Junr.	"
James Martin	Bangor	Andrew Kenmaer	Broom-Hedy
Alex. Ritchie	"	Samuel Piper	Menmeyre
Stephen Stewart	England	Robert Wilson,	
Stephan Stewart	"	wife and three	
Thomas Donaldson	Cooper in Fife,	children	Dunmurry
Henry Scott	" Scotland	Elizabeth Wilson	"
Daniel Aiken	Glasgow, Scotland		

(a) Ship Protection, Captain Bearns, 29 days from Belfast, landed at Amboy before April 20, 1811.

(b) Of the passengers, there were:

2	between	5 and 10 years old,
16	"	10 and 20 inclusive
43	"	20 and 30 "
12	"	30 and 40 "
-	"	40 and 50 none
3	"	50 and 60 inclusive
1	of	70
1	of	72
79,	chiefly farmers, and some with considerable property in guineas.	

(c)

Patrick M'Cartney	Banbridge	James Taylor	Armagh
Eliza M'Cartney	"	Louisa Taylor	"
Ellen M'Cartney	"	Jane M'Wherter	Newry
Catherine Parker	"	David Bell	Lisburn
Mary Sinclaire	"	Margaret Bell	"
James Ferris	"	James Bell	"
William Gordon	"	Henry Brown	"
Easter Gordon	"	Rachel Brown	"
Sarah Bryans	Moy	James Ross	Killinchy
John Gamble	Ballybay	Thomas M'Kee	Newtownards
Eliza Gamble	"	Margaret M'Kee	"
James Gamble	"	Robert M'Kee	"
William Gamble	"	Samuel M'Cartney	Banbridge
Joseph Gamble	"	Hannah M'Cartney	"
George Gamble	"	John Sinclaire	"
John Morron	"	Anne Sinclaire	"
Bell Gamble	"	Eliza M'Mullan	Larne
William Clement	"	Patrick M'Kee	Armagh
John Smyth	Downpatrick	Easter Teas	Belfast
James Glas	Belfast	Margaret Watt	Banbridge
Nevin See	Ballybay	Haney M'Comb	Keady
Owen Maron	Ballytrea	Ann M'Comb	"
Christopher Banecan	"	Margaret M'Comb	"
Samuel Magell	Banbridge	Thomas M'Comb	"
Ellen Magell	"	John M'Whatey	Armagh
John Magell	"	Jane M'Whatey	"
Robert Forsyth	"	Alexander M'Kenny	Bangor
Valentine Forsyth	"	James Pinkerton	Killinchy
Mary Forsyth	"	Thomas Hamilton	Antrim
Robert Forsyth	"	John Conaghy	"
John Forsyth	"	Robert Douglass	Ballymena
Sarah Forsyth	"	Ann Bunham	Newry
George Irwine	Waringstown	Wm. Patterson	Bangors
George Irwine	"	Eliza Patterson	"
Rachel Irwine	"	John Andrews	Combers
Robert M'Cracken	Ballymacaret	Hugh M'Cawley	Crumlin
John Hanry	Rathfreland	Mathw. M'Cully	"
William Carse	Killinchy	Robert Sterling	Doagh
Robert Hamilton	Cumber	James Sterling	"
		James Watt	Lisburn

(a) Ship Radius, Captain Clark, from Cork, arrived at New York before May 11, 1811.

(c) The list includes passengers' names and places of nativity.

Miles Kirkby	----	Jerry Malowney	Agtis
Edward Lewis	London	John Malowney	"
Daniel Philips	"	Edmund Murry	"
Jacob Gulich	Hamburg	Margaret Maloney	"
Philip Gulich	"	Bridget Gallivan	Cappequin
James Tuffnell	London	John Cunningham	"
Hugh Parker	Cork	Frances Cunningham	"
Hugh Sadler	"	Michael Cavanaugh	"
Frances Sadler	"	Peter Slattery	"
Samuel Freeman	Waterford	Margaret Slattery	"
David M'Kardy	Dungannon	John Slattery	Lismore
John Bull	Kilkenny	William Divine	Tullow
Jane Hannah	London	Redmond Kent	Lismore
Mary Connor	Cork	John Kearceay	"
Jeremiah Connor	"	Thomas Kearceay	"
Eliza Kirby	"	Margaret Kearceay	"
Cornelius Kirby	"	Patrick Foaley	"
Mary Ann Kirby	"	John Callihan	Tallow
Margaret Keane	"	Luke Linnen	Cappaquin
Richard Carey	"	Henry O'Brien	Clonmell
Thomas Rice	"	Massy Haskett	Burris O'Kean
Thomas Fowey	Castlelions	Richard Haskett	"
Timothy Murphy	"	Michael Kearney	"
Robin Pigott	Castlehyde	Thomas Rian	"
James Barry	Youghal	James Guess	"
Thomas M'Key	Fermoy	Thomas Dunnahough	Narragh
Elley M'Key	"	John Lane	Clonmell
Henry Bullen	Clonikelty	Mary Lane	"
Mary Bullen	"	Catherine Buckley	"
John Leaky	Glanmire	Ellen Lane	"
James Sanders	"	John Blake	Emily
John Ranihan	Cork	John Casey	----
James Barry	Watergroshill	Francis Kearney	Birr
Stephen Cronin	Castlemartyr	John Gunn	Castlereagh
James Fogerty	Dungarvin		

(a) The Algernon, Captain Nathan Clark, departed Belfast on April 10, arrived at New York on May 9, 1811.

(b) Commendation of Capt. Clark signed by: George Thompson
    William Orr
    Henry M'Curry
    William Coburn
    Robert Hall

Of the passengers there were: 42 under 10 years of age
    38 between 10 and 20
    36 between 20 and 30
    19 between 30 and 40
    8 between 40 and 50
    5 between 50 and 60
    148

(c)

Robert Lowry and family	Charlemont	Wm. Orr and family	Hill Hall
Alex Beally and family	Hillsborough	John Orr and family	Hill Hall
Wm. and Eliza Armstrong	Co. Down	Mary Nixon, George Nixon and family	Kill Warlin
John Neilson and family	Co. Down	Ann Coin and children	Belfast
James Tate	Maze	Hobert Hall and family	Belfast
Robert Hasby	"	Wm. Coborn and family	Kill Warlin
James Kennecy	Halls Mill	Henry M'Curry, Mary M'Curry, A. Carlton	Hillsborough
John and Mary Hamilton	Hillsborough		
James Amberson	Halls Mill		
John Gurley and family	Co. Down	John Wall and family, Easter Wall	Banbridge
Hamilton M'Cullough	Co. Tyrone	Samuel Gelison and family	Co. Down
Edward Pepper and family	Moyallen	Samuel Burns	Halls Mills
James and Sarah M'Connell	Hill Hall	Mary Sinton and family	Moyallen
Richard Hinds and family	Dromore	James Camble	Ballynahinch
Wm. Copeland and family	Co. Down	James Deek, Agnes Deek	"
James Morrison and family	Armagh	John and Susan Smith	"
Ellen Tetterson, Robert Tetterton and family	Banford	George Thompson	Belfast
		John Maguinis, Isabella Maguinis	Co. Down
John Bonnel	Queen's County	John Morrison	Magheragel
John Morrow	Banford	Sally Green	Lurgan
Edward Dial and family	Rathfreland	John Lamb	Maze
		James Meharg	Co. Down
Robert and Rachel Kennedy	Banford	Sarah M'Mahan	Dromore
		Joseph Mark	"

(a) The Westpoint, Captain Boggs, 36 days from Londonderry, landed at New York before May 25, 1811, with 105 passengers.

(b) "We regret that none of the lists of passengers which we have seen contain their places of residence in Ireland, nor could we possibly procure this information from themselves, as they scattered in every direction immediately after landing."

(c)

John Lambert	Eliza Marshall	Thos. M'Menamy
Henry Lenon	George Marshall	Jos. M'Menamy
John Dougherty	JohnnM'Cready	Robt. M'Elkeney
Edward Rice	Nath. M'Caghy	James Brown
Margaret Christie	and family	Mgt. M'Mennamy
and child	James Steel	Wm. M'Mennamy
John O'Neill	Michael Hamard	Michael Denvant
Philip M'Laughlin	Math. Kirkpatrick	James Ward
Ann M'Laughlin	John M'Kinlay	Connel Sweeny
Martha Slone	George M'Kinlay	Peter Lyons
Rob't Thompson	Edward Hamilton	Cornelius Lyons
Thomas Russell	Jane Doneil	Isaac Vance
James Russell	Dennis Hanagan	William Brown
John Hamilton	James Dougherty	D. Vance
Benjamin M'Lary	James Piden	Charles Logan
Samuel Gilmer	Thomas Freeborn	Rebecca Crawford
John Madden	and family	Hugh Strong
Margaret Hanlan	Patrick Kearny	Chr. Strong
and family	James Carrigan	Cath. Graham
James Grey	Wm. Carrigan	and family
Catherine Kerr	Henry Scott	John Smiley
and family	Alexander Scott	Wm. Thompson
Benj. M'Laughlin	Andrew Funston	Susan M'Cafferty
Conell Curry	Ar. Donaghy	William Porter
Geo. M'Caughall	Roger M'Guire	John Hutton
Corn. M'Ginley	Patterson Jolly	John Campbell
W. Marshall	John Hamill	A. Witherington
and family	Mary M'Gohey	Elizabeth Miligan
Joseph Marshall		

(a) The Jupiter, Captain William H. Hutchins or Hitchins, from Belfast, landed at New York before June 1, 1811.

(b) Commendation of the captain signed by:

Thomas Stephens	James M'Tier	John Glass
David M'Meehan	Thos. Harrison	Patrick Sweeny
Wm. Anderson	Thos. M'Vea	Edward Catton
Chris. Cassidy	James M'Alpin	Robert Patrick

(c) Passengers' names and residences:

Hugh Johnson	Hillsborough	Elizabeth Hamilton	Molany
Elizabeth Johnson	"	James Gallery	Moreyrea
Matthew Murdough	Moira	Eliza Gallery	"
William Harshaw	Down	William M'Kelery	"
John M'Coskery	"	Jane M'Kelery	"
John Boyd	"	John Ewart	"
John M'Kee	Magradill	James Kearns	Aghadie
Jane M'Kee	"	Elizabeth Kearns	"
Hugh Perry	Cullsallag	Andrew George	Killead
Margaret Perry	"	William George	"
David Evart	"	Martha George	"
Arthur Deolin	"	Mark M'Atter	Blaris
Joseph Camble	Dungannon	Betty M'Atter	"
John Turkenton	"	Alexander Mention	"
James Turkenton	"	Agnes Mention	"
Jane Turkenton	"	William Reid	Cumber
Thomas Dixon	"	James Gelston	"
Joanna Dixon	"	Thomas Stephans	"
John Clark	Lurgan	Elnor Stephans	"
Thomas M'Dowl	Saintclaire	David M'Magun	Banbridge
John M'Dowl	"	Seragh M'Magan	"
Alexander M'Dowl	"	Agnus M'Magan	"
Elizabeth M'Dowl	"	William Anderson	"
Rachel M'Dowl	"	Catherine Anderson	"
Mary Ann M'Dowl	"	Samuel Jameson	Killinchie
Thomas Fair	"	Agnus Jameson	"
Ann Fair	"	Bernard Conaghy	Banbridge
James Fair	"	John M'Kee	Ballinahinch
Patrick Sweeny	Ballinahinch	Charles M'Carton	"
William Sweeny	"	James M'Carton	"
Prudence Sweeny	"	Samuel Gamble	"
Edward Patton	Grable	Robert Patrick	Belfast
John Glass	"	Daniel Deolin	Banbridge
John Johnson	Antrim	George Best	"
Elnor Johnson	"	Seragh Best	"
David Johnson	"	Alexander M'Dowl	Ilandery
Elizabeth Johnson	"	Ezibella M'Dowl	"
William Chaley	"	Thomas Harrison	Cairn
James M'Alpin	Molany	Jane Harrison	"
Jane M'Alpin	"	James M'Attur	Killead
Hugh M'Alpin	"	Ann M'Attur	"
Conway Hamilton	"	John Metchon	"
Margaret Hamilton	"	Seragh Rhea	"

David Rhea	Killead	Thomas Phillips	Glenary
Samuel Stephenson	"	Eliza Phillips	"
Thomas M'Key	Dunleery	James M'Mullen	Tyrone
Samuel Cleland	"	Eliza M'Mullen	"
Henry Cook	Armagh	Robert M'Mullen	"
John Stephanson	"		

11-9

(a) Brig Orlando, Captain Josiah Cromwell, 31 days from Belfast, landed at New York on May 19, 1811, with 55 passengers.

(b) See 11-7 (b).

(c)
John Davison and family	Richard Hughes and family	John Quin and family
Thomas Kennedy	James Brady and family	Henry M'Mahon
James Frasier	Robert M'Cane	James Ker
Robert Frasier	Thomas Stark	Thomas Sherran
Mary Russell	William Munn and family	James Henderson and family
Jas. Morrow and family	Rachel Hun	James Anderson
Wm. Maxwell	James Thompson	John Cannon
Ann Patterson	Marg't Thompson	William Burns
Mary Logan	Henry Johnston and family	Elizabeth Burns
James Little	Felix M'Allisted	John Owens
Henry Drake	James M'Allisted	James Johnson
Thomas W. Ray		Jane Morrow
		Anna Dreison

11-10

(a) The Mary Augusta, Captain Hall, 37 days from Newry, arrived at New York before May 25, 1811 with 102 passengers.

(b) "Exclusive of the passengers per the Westpoint, a list of whom we give today, we are glad to perceive Captain Alexander and Mrs. Thompson, Mr. and Mrs. Bonner and Miss Jane Bonner." These passengers appear on none of the published lists and so evidently were aboard the Mary Augusta.

(c) No list published.

11-11

(a) Ship Aeolus, Captain Charles Henry, 35 days from Newry, arrived at New York on May 23, 1811 with 80 passengers.

(b) See 11-7(b).

(c)

John Fulton and family	Betsey M'Cabe	Francis Henrietta
Moore M'Donald	F. M'Laughlin and family	Frances Henrietta
Samuel Hunter and family	John M'Gurrah and family	John Kell
William Clark	George Lemman	John Hughes
John Seave and family	Mary Lemman	James Copeland
Samuel M'Murry and family	John Thompson and family	Thomas Copeland
William Boyd and family	James Moore	John Sewere
John Harshaw and family	Samuel Crary	Francis Devan
Joseph Fleman	Elizabeth Smith and family	Eliza Lister and child
Betsey Fleman	Mary Armstrong and child	Agnes Carver
Jane Sleeman	John Hunter	John Barker
John Walker and family	Abraham Keating	James Bell
James M'Cabe	Thomas Seeman	Joseph Douglass
	Peter Grabbin	Betsey Hetherton
	Edward DeHart	William Ballah
		James M'Steeve
		Isaac Armstrong
		Margaret Moore

11-12

(a) Ship Erin, Captain O'Conner, 40 days from Dublin, arrived at New York before June 1, 1811. No mention of passengers.

11-13

(a) Ship John Watson, from Dublin, arrived at New York about May 30, 1811. No mention of passengers.

(a) Ship Africa, Captain John E. Scott, from Belfast, arrived at New York on June 9, 1811.

(c) Passengers' names and birthplaces:

George Roberts	Armagh	John Patterson	Belly Keell
Samuel M'Cammar	"	Arthur Shee	Rathfriland
William Murphy	Monagher	William Willis	Dungannon
Mary Murphy	"	Felix Farren	"
John Hawthorn	Billikiel	Margaret Willis	"
Agnes Hawthorn	"	Sally Farren	"
David Scott	"	James Farren	"
Margaret Scott	"	Thomas Kelly	"
John Logan	"	Molly Kelly	"
Jacob Pierson	Armagh	Hugh Cunningham	Rathfriland
Jane Pierson	"	Michael M'Anorney	"
Margaret Moffit	"	Patrick Mancey	"
James Rock	"	Jane M'Faden	Hillsborough
Mary Rock	"	John Buchannon	Carrickfergus
Joseph Bridget		Samuel Irvine	
and family	Balleck	and family	Dunganon
John M'Cullaugh		William Gatt	"
and family	Carmer	John M'Cartney	Loughbrickland
William Heson	"	Nancy M'Cartney	"
William Spratt	"	James Bodd	"
Mary Spratt	"	James M'Curtney	"
William Shaw	Billamegary	Martha Heran	"
Margaret Shaw	"	James Herker	Belfast
John Porter	"	William Quail	
Eliza Fullan	Lisburn	and family	Downpatrick
Scalion Fullan	"	William Stockdale	"
Andrew Martin	Kilmore	Jane Stockdale	"
Jane Morrow	Monaghan	Jane Warren	Belfast
Ellen Morrow	"	Hugh Warren	"
Jane Morrow	"	Ann Aiken	Dromore
John Finlay	"	Jane Aiken	"
James Cowser	"	John Cleland	Lisburn
William M'Caird	"	Wm. Armstrong	Down
Sophia Cowser	Armagh	Arabella Armstrong	"
Eliza Cowser	"	Wm. Armstrong	"
Jane Cowser	"	Eleanor Blany	"
Hugh O'Ray	Belfast	Joseph Patterson	"
John Gruir		David Patterson	
and family	Belfast	and family	Down
Robert Noore	Dungannon	Mary Patterson	"
Eliza Moore	"	Wm. Willis	"
Thomas Moore		James White	"
and family	Rathfriland	Robert Burk	"
Thomas Calvin	"	Edward Hazleton	"
William Forcade		James Morgan	
and family	Belfast	and family	Down
Henry Moore	Rathfriland	George Patterson	"
Mary Moore	"	Eliza Thompson	"

11-14, continued

Maria Thompson	Down	Joseph Thompson	Down
Sarah Thompson	"	John Hodgson	"
John Thompson	"	John Lockat	"
James Thompson	"	John Fulton	Lisburn
George Thompson	"		

11-15

(a) Ship Alexandria, Captain Edmund Fanning, from Londonderry, arrived at New York on June 12, 1811 with 85 passengers and their families.

(c)
Robert Potts
  and family
David Hanshaw
George Cobine
Robert Cobine
Joseph Akin
Mary Akin
Felix O'Neal
John Huges
William Akin
James Foster
Mary Foster
Margaret Foster
Andrew Robinson
  and family
John Foster
James Stewart
John Carson
Joseph Michell
John Hinds
Hugh Dolonson
  and family
Hugh M'Kosker
Edward Harver
Margaret Akin
James Robston
James Given
John Hutchin Junr.
Margaret Givin
Daniel Killy
Patrick Quin

James Smyth
John Foster
John Hall
Charles Vimmo
Eliza Vimmo
Edward Doholy
Neal Dougherty
Nancy Clark
Thomas Neilson
William Neilson
Hugh Harkin
Neal M'Lorlan
Patrick M'Lorlan
Neal Kelly
Patrick Cannon
William George
  and family
John George
  and family
William Elliot
John Given
Elizabeth Miller
Mary Ann Dixon
John Aikens
Thomas Dixon
Robert Kelly
Robert Miller
John Stevenson
John Scott
William Young

Robert Mansfield
Andrew Collins
James Coslarder
William Smith
Andrew Lindsay
Isabella Lindsay
Charles M'Feely
Michael Gillespie
Fanny Gillespie
Philip Dougherty
William Dougherty
Daniel M'Faul
William Stevenson
Wil. Mathewson
Fanny Young
Owen Mechan
Catherine Mechan
John Boyd
James M'Anulty
James Murry
George Carson
James Carson
William Nelson
Gerard Nelson
Robert Hunter
Ann Hunter
John Little
  and family
Mary Clark
John Nelson

11-16

(a) The Golconda, from Londonderry, arrived at New York before June 15, 1811.

(c) Robert Philson
John Fletcher
John Duffey
Alex. Smiley
James Smiley
Daniel Kirr
James Shawkling
Dudly Dougherty
Dennis Boyle
John Cannon
John Caldwell
  and family
Marg. Alexander
Alex. Glass
Isabella Glass
Francis Minetes
Biddy Minetes
Mary Haggerty
Barney Donald
James Burnes
Murphy Burns
John M'Faden
John M'Conlay
Danl. M'Ginness
William Crone
Michael Donald
Eleanor Donald
Mary Atkins
John Mollony
Darby Burns

Peter Haughey
Dan. Cunningham
John Rodgers
John Burns
  and family
David Stewart
William Henry
Jacob Giller
John Kerr
Benjamin Haughey
John M'Colley
Henry Burns
John White
Thomas Burns
Thomas Faren
Coudy Cunningham
Mary Rodgers
Patrick Barney
Michael Manely
Henry Manely
William Hickings
Patrick Hickings
Michael Hagerty
Daniel Hagerty
John Burns
  and family
Timothy Timons
Isabella Timons
Jeremiah Starr

Ralph Waddel
Rodger Murry
John Rudder
Patrick Rudder
John M'Greedy
Edw. M'Conway
John Fanan
Catherine Burns
James Burns
Marg. M'Grave
William Pollock
Samuel Pollock
John M'Mannyman
Philip Carling
Edward M'Ganty
Samuel Johnson
Dominick Golley
Thomas Scott
J. Cunningham
C. Cunningham
Robert Lyons
Bany Traner
Thomas Burns
  and family
John Hazelton
Jacob Bell
Mary Bell
John Fanen
Tames Taylor

11-17

(a) Brig Patty, Captain Sawer, from Newry, arrived at Philadelphia on
Sunday June 16, 1811.

(c) Wm. Nelson
  and family   Drumduff
John Nelson
  and family   Drumduff
John Marks
  and family   Armagh
Thos. Gorman
  and family   Castleblany

H. M'Quillin
  and family   Downpatrick
William Seed   "
James English   "
Richard Corney   "
Elizabeth Donnell   Armagh
William Davis   Coleraine
James Sweeney   Londonderry
---- Ferguson   Belfast

(a) Ship Mary, Captain Wallington, from Londonderry, arrived at Philadelphia on June 17, 1811.

(b) "Mr. John Moorhead, who is mentioned as drowned, was lost near the Lazaretto. The particulars are not mentioned. The captain says he was a very fine young man." The Lazaretto was a quarantine station and hospital near Philadelphia.

(c)

Thos. M'Grath	Barnard Davis	James Hunter
Marg. M'Grath	Joseph Magis	Wm. Hunter
James M'Grath	Sarah Wishat	Eleanor Hunter
Martha Smith	Mary Wishat	Samuel Glen
Wm. Key	Ruth Wishat	James Thompson
Wm. Craig	Sarah Wishat	Patrick Crosson
Elizabeth Morrison	Margaret Duncan	James Woods
Martha Morrison	George Williams	Joseph Tagart
John Moorhead	Charles Hamilton	Patrick M'Leon
(Drowned)	Daniel Hamilton	Jane M'Brine
Sam'l Wallace	Robert Wishat	Ann Brown
Wm. Ceyrin	David M'Knight	Patrick Connelly
Wm. Williams	Mary M'Knight	Pat. M'Gellaghan
John Cummings	Andrew M'Knight	Alex. Larkie
Z. Bennett	Jane M'Knight	Mary Larkie
Nathan Rogers	Thomas M'Knight	Robert Norris
Wm. Beatty	Daniel M'Knight	Mary Norris
Jane Beatty	Francis Monegan	Cornelius Crossen
George Beatty	James Gillaspie	Catherine Doyle
William Clark	Terrence M'Lorten	Abrm. M'Intire
Ann Clark	Cather. M'Lorten	John Rein
David Clark	Harvey Roulston	John Clarey
Eleanor Ross	Martha Roulston	John Thorne
Joseph Ross	James Roulston	James Fee
Wm. Hamilton	Arthur Wason	Antho. Campbell
James Edmundon	Jane Wason	Gabriel Andrews
Adam Woods	Sarah Curragan	Andrew Mills
David Harvey	James Fife	Francis Maze
Thos. Dougherty	Joseph Douglass	James Laverty
Abigail Dougherty	Laurin Fothall	Patrick Fee
Patrick Flanagan	Mary Genagul	Anthony Mulden
William Ross	William M'Curdy	Jane Lurkie
Andrew Gibson	Morgan M'Curdy	

(a) Ship Shamrock, Captain M'Keon, from Dublin, arrived at New York before June 29, 1811 with 60 passengers and their families.

(b) "Many of the passengers per the Shamrock and Huntress, are very respectable, and none under the degree of mechanics and farmers. Not one servant of either sex could be obtained from amongst them."

(c) Passengers' names and places of birth:

Edward Caffrey	Queen's Co.	Nicholas Sinnot	Wicklow
Morris Fitzgerald	Dublin	James M'Key	Tipperary
Mark Pigott	Carlow	Wm. Reynolds	King's Co.
Matthew Kelly	Kilkenny	John Carrall	Tipperary
William Walsh	"	Thomas Murtagh	Drogheda
John Scully	Burris a Kane	Michael Kelly	"
Timothy Murphy	King's Co.	Brien Reilly	Castle Pollard
John Stockdale	Dublin	Wm. Ryan	Dublin
Miles Byrne		M. Erraty	
and family	Dublin	and family	Kilkenny
Matthey Murphy	"	John M'Evory	Dublin
Wm. Fitzpatrick	Queen's Co.	Benjamin Wilson	New York, U.S.A.
G. Edwards		Wm. Thompson	Philadelphia, U.S
and family	Dublin	Mary M'Clane	Cavan
John Laplin	Kilkenny	John Bradley	Tipperary
James Ryan	Queen's Co.	Henry Withers	Dublin
J. Shinluig		Michael Alchorn	Philadelphia, U.S
and family	Antrim	Patrick Rorke	Tipperary
Richard Hallugan	Co. Louth	Patrick Sherlock	Dublin
Henry Colin	"	John Wright	"
Andrew Daye	Queen's Co.	Eliza Wright	"
James Trenar	"	James Kerwan	Castle Pollard
Patrick Trenar	"	Wm. M'Grath	Drogheda
James Durham	Dublin	Thomas Corcoran	Dublin
Margaret Durham	"	Wm. Corcoran	"
Henry Stephenson	"	Michael Leary	Castle Pollard
T. Fitzpatrick		John M'Clane	Co. Cavan
and family	Caven	Mary M'Clane	"
Thomas Phelan	Kilkenny	Peter Philar	Queen's Co.
John Platt	Youghill	James Ryan	Dublin
Themas Ryan	Tipperary	Catherine Wright	Cavan
David Ryan	"	Wm. Stanley	
Thomas Delany	Wexford	and family	Dublin

(a) Ship Huntress, Captain Thomas Ronson, from Dublin, arrived at New York on June 24, 1811 with 47 passengers and their families.

(b) See 11-19(b).
Commendation of Captain Ronson signed by Joshua Craig, John Field, and Peter Kenny.
Passenger Thomas M'Cormick, age 20, died in the period July 3 - July 7, 1811, of the intense heat in New York city.

(c)

John Field	Dublin	Patrick Meeghan	Tipperary
Peter Kenney	"	M. Flanery	
Catherine Kenney	"	and family	Tipperary
Jos. Craig		N. Carden	
and family	Dublin	and family	Tipperary
Chas. Craig		Margaret Phelan	"
and family	Dublin	John Cullin	Kilkenny
John Craig	"	Patrick Cancannon	"
George Echard	"	Patrick Lawler	Wexford
Peter Toole	"	John Doyle	"
John Armitage	Tipperary	John Murphy	"
John Horan	King's Co.	Michael Doyle	"
John Horan	Tipperary	Patrick Finney	"
T. Kinch		Matthew Finney	"
and family	Wexford	John Dealy	"
James Kinch	"	Thomas M'Cormick	Longford
John Stout	"	George Lanigan	"
John Keating	Dublin	Patrick Forley	Cavin
Mary Keating	"	William Ryan	Tipperary
M. Gregory		Thomas Davis	Wicklow
and family	Meath	Edward Clark	Caven
John Gregory	Co. Louth	Owen Gerighaty	Meath
Bridget Harman	"	Martin Justin	Queen's Co.
Thomas Branigon	"	Henry Sutliff	"
Michael Devine	"	Edward Sutliff	"
Susan Gunea	Dublin	Betsy Lucus	"
James Byrne	Wicklow		

11-21

(a) Ship Hibernia, Captain Graham, 34 days from Belfast, arrived at New York or June 28 or 29, 1811 with 100 passengers.

(c)

Francis Kane and family	J. Dickson and family	Mrs. Emerson and family
Patrick Reid	John Jameson	James Gordon
John Armstrong	James Walker	and family
George Mulholland	and family	Wm. Paine
John Shaw	Charles Leviston	and family
David Brown and family	Mary Leviston	Susanna Hayson
Keziah Blythe	Rachel Wylie	David Reed
Mary Guiy	James M'Donnell and family	Margaret Reed
Margaret Guiy	P. M'Connell	James Creckan
Josias Currie	and family	Augustus Henry
Wm. Flemming	Thomas Martin	Wm. Hutchison
James Cochlin	and family	Robert M'Comb and family
Richard Harper	John Thompson and family	A. Scott
Jane Harper	Dennis Keenan	James Lockery
Catherine Harper	Hugh Keenan	Margaret Lockery
Joseph Harper	James M'Kie	James Leviston and family
Samuel Harris	John Robeson	Alex. M'Conaghy
Mary Harris	Thomas M'Cloy and family	Jos. MieKin
Hugh Fergusson	Hugh M'Ildoon	James Maffett
Wm. M'Culloch	Wm. Hartley	R. M'Allister
Mary M'Culloch	Hugh Tracy	Rose M'Allister
Robert Service	James Molineauo	John Dick
Jas. M'Connaghy	Daniel Lynn and family	M. George
M. M'Vey and family		Samuel Hall
Wm. Hurley		Alexander George
J. Hurley		Eliza George

11-22

(a) The Washington, Captain West, 35 days from Londonderry, arrived at New York before July 5, 1811 with 119 passengers.

(c) No list published.

11-23

(a) The Friendship, Captain Harrison, from Kinsale, arrived at New York before July 5, 1811; no mention of passengers.

(a) The Belisarius, Captain Morgan, 42 days from Dublin, arrived at New York before July 5, 1811.

(b) "The unfortunate circumstance of the latter having met with the British ship of war Atalanta, on the western border of George's Bank, has been announced in other papers. Among the multifarious acts of British cruelty there will be found few to equal in atrocity the forcing from on board the Belisarius, 62 Irish passengers, consisting of men, women and children. A gentleman by the Belisarius gives us a most feeling description of this distressing scene: the shrieks of the unfortunate parties on being dragged into the boats, - the lamentations of the aged parents who were left behind, - the wife clinging to her husband, - the child grasping the knee of its more than distracted father, on giving up his last hope to provide for his little ones, and doomed to serve his tyrants - all con- contributed to render the scene truly one of the most distressing which ever occurred. ...yet we are concerned to state that we have met with some who justify this iniquitous transaction, on the ground that those passengers who were taken did not clear out or pass the custom-house. This assertion we are authorized to say is false, as their names were on the custom-house return - some small children excepted. In the list of passengers will be found the names designated of the unfortunate people who were taken." This list is that of (c) below. The event took place on June 24, 1811.

The story is continued in the Shamrock of August 10, 1811: "We are happy to announce the safe arrival in this city of Messrs. Patrick and William Phelan, two of the persons taken in June last from the ship Bellisarius, on her passage from Dublin to this port, by his Britannic majesty's sloop of war Atalanta.

"We are indebted to Mr. W. Phelan for the following account of the fate of the persons taken as above, which we publish for the information of their friends here.

"On the arrival of the Atalanta at Halifax, the following persons and their families, consisting of forty-three individuals, were removed to a sloop, which sailed with them to the island of St. John's, with directions that they should be put on the estate of Lord James Townshend.

Richard King	Eliza Birk	Cath. Needham
Jane King	Thomas Walsh	Eliza Needham
James King	Thomas Newman	Joseph Gilbert
Mary King	Lawrence Current	Ann Gilbert
Jane King	Thomas Bird	Ally Burton
John Gilbert	Mary Bird	Michael Murphy
John Birk	Valient Needham	

"The following seventeen persons were continued on board the Atalanta, and are now probably employed in endeavors to snatch others of their friends or countrymen from a prospect of peace, liberty, and independence, to wear out life in an inhospitable clime and under the guidance of some absentee or unmerciful landlord; or unwillingly to aid in supporting the British claim to the exclusive sovereignty of the ocean.

Richard Langer	Edward Dore	Bartlet Turner
Peter Foley	William Morgan	Edward Lacey
James Graham	Peter Courtney	Thomas Walsh
John Dunn	Michael M'Holland	Martin Bambrick
James Costigan	Mathew Murphy	Michael Bambrick
William Turner	William Sutton	

Peter Foley, one of the above, having feigned illness, with a view to effect his discharge, the physician of the Atalanta said he would administe a remedy which would cure him if really ill, and force him to confess, if only pretendedly so;...

"The Messrs. Phelans were permitted to land, on condition of remaining for life at Halifax; but conceiving that an engagement under such circumstances, and made to such a government, not binding in honor, they took an early opportunity of breaking their parole, and, after passing from place to place and from ship to ship, at length reached this city, the place of their original destination.

...."But Lord Townshend's estate in the cold island of St. John's must for ever remain uncultivated but for this expedient."

(c)

Richard King	Edward Dove	Edward Lacy
Jane King	William Turner	The above were all taken.
James King	William Morgan	James Charowell
Mary King	Lawrence Current	Dennis Menteur
Jane King and	Peter Courtney	Robert Hughs
five children	Mich. M'Holland	and family
Richard Langer	Thomas Bird	Wm. Nailor
Benjn. Tukerbury	Mary Bird	and family
and family	Valient Needham	Jane Connor
Peter Folly	Catherine Needham	and family
William Phelan	Eliza Needham	Martin Baimbrick
Patrick Phelan	Mathew Murphy	and family
James Graham	Joseph Gilbert	William M'Donald
Bartlett Turner	Ann Gilbert	Stephen Mathews
John Gilbert	Ally Burton	and wife
Mary Ann Gilbert	Patrick Pierce	Henry Stanhope
John Birk	Michael Murphy	and wife
Eliza Birk	and family	William Harding
Thomas Walsh	William Sutton	and wife
Thomas Newan	John Dunn	Rev. Mr. Ryan
James Costagan		

1-25

(a) Ship Joseph and Phoebe, Captain Plympton, from Londonderry, arrived at
Baltimore on July 4, 1811.

(c)

Armstrong Walker	Francis Cassidy	Ann Porter
William Shaw	James M'Nought	Thomas Porter
John Dougherty	John Brogan	Elizabeth Porter
Owen Dougherty	John Murdock	Bell Porter
Thomas Fulton	Esther Murdock	William Anderson
Mary Dogherty	M. Anne Murdock	Esther M'Cousland
Philip Dogherty	Margaret O'Brien	Mary M'Cousland
Biddy Dogherty	Owen O'Brien	Mar. M'Cousland
Cathar. Dogherty	Catherine Tonner	Ann M'Cousland
Mary Dogherty	John Dury	John Sproul
Isaac Dogherty	John Floyd	Jane Conn
Tobt. Thompson	Samuel Lyons	Samuel Conn
Charles M'Ilroy	Catherine Boyle	Robert Conn
William Anthony	John Boyle	Sarah Conn
James Gatt	Margaret Owins	Thomas Wilson
John Glinchy	James Owins	Sarah Espy
John Stevenson	James Young	Eliza Kane
Martha Stevenson	Ann Finnegan	Mary Lyons
William Haslam	John Murdock	James Lyons
Margaret Haslam	Saml. Crummer	Joseph Lyons
Robert Henderson	Cathar. Crummer	John Lyons
William Henderson	Nathl. Crummer	Eliza Lyons
Marg. Henderson	Ann Crummer	Eliza Crosier
John Harshaw	Mary Crummer	Barney Birns
Margaret Harshaw	Letitia Crummer	Frank M'Neal
William Harshaw	Hamill Pollock	William Barns
Pat. Donaghy	James Woods	Stephen Connel
John M'Creery	Terance Duvas	Thomas M'Cue
Robert Griffith	James Watson	Barney Donaghey
Jane Griffith	James Wilson	George Dogherty
Mary Griffith	Geo. M'Cullock	Charles Adams
William Duddy	John Russel	Anthony M'Gill
Henry Duddy	Terance Boyle	James Scott
William M'Ever	John Porter	Alex. M'Caughan

11-26

(a) Ship Rising States, Captain Stilwell, from Newry, arrived at Philadelphia on July 8, 1811.

(c) Wm. Montgomery
and family
Joseph Montgomery
and family
James Scott
and family
Patrick Tweedy
and family
James Murry
and family
Michael Henry
and family
James M'Clenaghan
Joseph Carr
Patrick Cassely
George Shields

Clem M'Cune
Robert Wharton
Bernard M'Ginnis
John Curry
John Glasgaw
Jane Egar
David Gibson
John Best
and family
Joseph Wharton
and family
Wm. Gibson
and family
Neil Boyle
and family

John Watt
and family
James Mahaffy
and family
John Dickson
Robert Gibson
Mrs. M'Burney
Alexander Gilloe
Nancy Riley
Margaret Riley
Thomas Hodgson
Mary Jackson
John Fitzsimons
Andrew Fitzsimmons

11-27

(a) The President, Captain Baker, from Newry, arrived at New York before July 13, 1811 with 92 passengers.

(c) No list published.

11-28

(a) The Massachusetts, Captain Stevens, from Dublin, arrived at New York before July 13, 1811; no mention of passengers.

11-29

(a) Brig Isaac, Captain Delano, 60 days from Cork, arrived at Philadelphia on Sunday, July 14, 1811.

(c) Passengers' names and residences:

Charles Harding	Cork
Michael Callaghan	Killarney
Mr. Wall	Clonmell
Capt. Graves	Philadelphia, U.S.
Mrs. Long	"
George Davis	"
John Nicholas and family	Donnraile

11-30

(a) Ship Medford, from Newry, arrived at Philadelphia before July 20, 1811 with an unspecified number of passengers.

(b) "Our correspondent informs us that she was boarded off the American coast by a British ship of war, and had nine young men pressed."

(c) No list published.

11-31

(a) Brig Juno, Captain Thompson, 56 days from Belfast, landed at New York before August 17, 1811 with 100 passengers.

(c)

David Young	nigh Charlemont	Nancy M'Murray	nigh Kilrea
John Malcomson	Portadown	two children M'Murray	"
James M'Glonan	Ballymoney	John Kerr	"
Ann M'Glonan-wife	"	Rachel Kerr-wife	"
Mary M'Glonan	"	Four children Kerr	"
Nathaniel M'Glonan	"	Mathew Moore	Straban
Edward Winters	Portadown	--- Moore-wife	"
Mary Winters-wife	"	Three children Moore	"
Arthur Hughes	Belfast	John Banner	Manchester, England
John Strean	nigh Dromore	Wm. -----	"
Edward Glenfuld	Lisburn	Neal M'Neill	Belfast
Robert Miller	Dungannon	Hugh Spratt	"
Matty Miller	"	John Gurry	nigh Downpatrick
John Derragh	Kilrea	his wife	"
Eliza Derragh	"	Wm. Law	Belfast
Ellen Derragh-child	"	* Hill Tollerton	nigh Soldierstown
John Pooler	Armagh	* Robert Watson	" "
Wm. Trimble	nigh Armagh	* Patrick Hagan	Castledawson
James Fullam	Magherafelt	* Mathew Shaw	nigh Connor
Ann Fullam	"	* Patrick M'Creely	Armagh
Wm. M'Murray	nigh Kilrea	* Robert ----	Manchester, England

Those marked * were pressed by the Strok sloop of war, when seven days out.

11-32

(a) Ship Mexicana, Captain Cook, 56 days from Dublin, arrived at Amboy before August 17, 1811 with 100 passengers.

(c) No list published.

11-33

(a) Brig Hespa, Captain Bailey, 55 days from Newry, arrived at New York between August 12 and August 17, 1811 with 62 passengers.

(b) On August 6, nine passengers were pressed out of her by the British sloop of war Eurydice.

(c) No list published.

11-34

(a) Ship Ariade, Captain Getty, of Boston, 45 days from Belfast, arrived at New York before August 31, 1811 with 114 passengers.

(c) No list published.

11-35

(a) Ship Ann, Captain Alexander Howland, 40 days from Londonderry, arrived at New York before August 31, 1811 with 36 passengers.

(c)

William Crow	James Eakins	John Johnston
Jane Crow	Rosannah Eakins	Margaret Wason
Margaret Crow	Margaret Eakins	and 4 children
Mathew Orr	Margaret Eakins jr.	John M'Farland
Alex. Armstrong	Sarah Eakins	wife & family
Jane Campbell	Rebecca M'Mahin	Margaret Farland
John Gray	P. Kirk	Wm. Buchanan
H. Weltch	John Jackson	George Wason
John & Margaret Vale	William Orr	Arm Armstrong

11-36

(a) Ship Jefferson, Captain Merryhew, 45 days from Londonderry, arrived at Amboy before August 31, 1811 with an unspecified number of passengers.

(c) No list published

11-37

(a) Ship Prosperity, from Londonderry, bound for Philadelphia with 130 passengers, spoken to by the Ship Ann four days before the Ann landed.

(c) No list published.

11-38

(a) Ship **Fame**, Captain William Pollock, 63 days from Londonderry, arrived at Philadelphia on August 31, 1811.

(c)
Samuel Torrers	James Arthur	John Alcorn
John Rutherford	Samuel Martin	and family
Mary Rutherford	James Martin	Francis Alcorn
Sarah Rutherford	Robert Orr	and wife
George Crockett	James Neilson	Charles Quinn
John Crockett	James Anderson	Samuel Dickey
Robert Crockett	James M'Connell	Nathaniel Dickey
George Smyth	Hugh M'Kinley	John Wilson
Arch. M'Elroy	George Culbert	Matthew Kerr
and family	George Crocket	James Dickey
Mrs. M'Togert	Samuel Crocket	John George
and family	Moses Hunter	Esther Bailey
Elizabeth Cross	John Kerr	James M'Closkey
Jane Simon	Robert Hector	Ruth Torrers
Martha Martin	James Grimes	Samuel Torrers
Rose Carolan	Robert M'Arthur	Ann Torrers
Martha Quigley	John M'Arthur	Samuel Rodgers
H. M'Laughlin	James Alcorn	Josua Orr
James Reed	Joseph Alcorn	

11-39

(a) Ship Boyne, departed Lough Swilly bound for Philadelphia before August 25, 1811.

(b) Carrying "over four hundred" passengers, the Boyne was turned back to Ireland by a British naval vessel, on the excuse of carrying seven children over the number allowed by British law for a ship of its size. The incident occurred before September 7.

11-40

(a) Ship Maria Duplex, 54 days from Belfast, landed at New York before September 21, 1811.

(c)
James Gray	Co. Antrim	Mrs. Bryson	Belfast
James Bennett	Co. Armagh	John Barr	
Dennis Carrall	Co. Tyrone	and family	Ballinahinch
John M'Bride, wife		Miss Mary Rodgers	Belfast
and family	Co. Down	Miss Susanna Bowen	"
Andrew Morran & wife	" "	William Quale	Downpatrick
John Walsh & wife	Dublin	Patrick Kelly	Dublin

(a) The Iris, from Newry, landed at Amboy before September 21, 1811 with an unspecified number of passengers.

(c) No list published.

11-42

(a) Ship Protection, Captain Bearns, 44 days from Belfast, landed at New York on September 20, 1811.

(c)

Name	Place	Name	Place
William Boyd	Killybegs	Joseph Verty	Penreth
Robert Cambell	Killinchy	Anthony Clothard	Kellenchy
Henry Atkinson	Dromore	Thomas Hamilton	Connors
Eliza Atkinson	"	Thomas M'Clure	Saintfield
James Atkinson	"	Robert J. Walker	Galway
Henry Atkinson	"	Robert M'Gaw	Stewartstown
Jane Atkinson	"	Thomas M'Gaw	"
Samuel Blair	Cullybickey	Anthony Bridge	Bedford, State of Pennsylvania
Eliza Blair	"		
William Gray	Armagh	Mary Campbell	Belfast
Jane Gray	"	Jemimah Campbell	"
Walter Gray	"	Samuel Booney	Greencastle
George Gray	"	Sarah Booney	"
Samuel Gray	"	Harriet Booney	"
John Gray	"	John Syllyman	Kellywaller
Elizabeth Gray	"	Billy Syllyman	"
Jane Gray	"	John P. Barron	New York
Thomas Davis	"	Effy Tweedy	Dromore
Thomas Preston	"	John Robinson	Wilsborough
John Wattsher	Tyrone	Jane Robinson	"
Ann Martin	Antrim	Thomas Robinson	"
Nancy Martin	"	Mary Robinson	"
James Luke	"	Hugh Neil	Crumlin
Jane Martin	Charlemont	John Wallace	Bangor
Isaac Cubbert	Armagh	Thomas Harris	Banbridge
Thomas Knox	Brougshane	John Quin	Antrim
William Knox	"	Margaret Quin	Antrim
Jane Knox	"	Jane Quin	"
Henry Williamson	Saintfield	Henry Quin	"
Elizabeth Williamson	"	James Thomson	Lisburn
Jane Williamson	"	Jane Thomson	"
Robert M'Donald	Portaferry	John Hughes	Bangor
Jane Knox	Brougshane	Jane Sloan	Doagh
Mathew Willis	Stewartstown	Jane Watt	Castlewillan
Mary Ann Willis	"	Hugh Laverty	Newtonards
Joseph Verty	Penreth	Jane Laverty	"

1-43

(a) The White Oak, from Dublin, arrived at New York before October 5, 1811.

(c)
James Hannah and family
John Bacon and family
---- Martin and family
---- Moran and family
----Cannon and family
William Kennedy and wife
---- Coe and sister
Dennis O'Brien

James Mullony
Mary M'Manus
* John Burke   near Mullingar
* Edward Smith   near Drogheda
* Another Englishman, name unknown
* Samuel Leech   Lancashire
* John Steel   Manchester
* Robert Steel   "

Those marked * were impressed by the Spartan frigate.

1-44

(a) Ship Mariner, 48 days from Londonderry, arrived at New London on September 21, 1811.

(c)
James Mubay and family	James Bryan and wife	Dennis Dogherty
Wm. M'Farland and family	M. Murphy and wife	David Arenner
David Virtue and family	S. Henderson	John Boyle
Archibald Elliott and family	William Scott	John Scanlon
Edward Dever and family	James Scott	Wm. Reynolds
Thomas Long and family	Richard Crozier	Mary Ross
Charles Kane and family	Eliz. Crozier	Anne Bryan
Robert M'Knott and family	P. M'Pharland	Alexander Carr
James Knox and family	Oliver Beatty	John Rafferty
Widow M'Pharland and 2 children	Ally Rice	Edward Timmory
Hugh Atcheson and wife	Maurice Ferry	Henry Williams
	John M'Askin	Alexander Hall
	John Alges	Robert Hall
	Thomas Hunter	John M'Ewen
	James Corrinn	Hugh Reed
	John M'Colgin	John Boyd
	John Moffit	Patrick Mathew
	William West	Patrick M'Grath
	David West	David Lindsay
		James Lindsay
		Torry Monogham

11-45

(a) Ship Caroline, Captain Ross, 65 days from Lough Swilly, arrived at New York before October 19, 1811 with 58 passengers.

(b) Originally bound for Philadelphia, she put into New York with her masts lost.

(c) No list published.

11-46

(a) Ship Fanny and Almira, Captain Ashby, 50 days from Belfast, landed at New York between October 13 and 26, 1811 with 30 passengers.

(b) On September 22 to the east of the banks, experienced a severe gale in which the rudder broke and could not be fixed until the 29th because of the gale wind from the west.
Was boarded on October 13 by the British brig Colibri, which pressed the following men:

James Service
T. Wylie
W. Kennedy
John Madden
Joseph M'Mullen
(above all tradesmen in steerage)
John M'Neill
J. Barnett
(above two cabin passengers)

(c) No list published.

11-47

(a) Ship Favourite, Captain Coles, 46 days from Dublin via Cork, arrived at New York on October 19, 1811 with 56 passengers.

(b) Forced into Cork by the British frigate Seldana, and detained for 12 days while the Captain proved that he was not carrying too many passengers.

(c) Cabin passengers: M. C. Murray
H. Shearman
J. O'Brien

11-48

(a) Ship Gleaner, Captain King, from Londonderry on September 5, arrived at Philadelphia on October 19, 1811 with 112 passengers.

(c) No list published.

11-49

(a) Brig Orlando, Captain Crowell, from Belfast, arrived in Barnstable, Massachusetts before October 26, 1811 with an unspecified number of passengers.

(c) No list published.

11-50

(a) The Keziah, from Belfast, arrived at New London before October 26, 1811 with an unspecified number of passengers.

(c) No list published.

11-51

(a) Ship Harmony, Captain Holkirk, 70 days from Londonderry, arrived at Philadelphia on October 31, 1811.

(b) Spoken to on September 25 by the Caroline; had lost mizen mast and fore and main top masts.

(c)

Edward Loughead	Mary Hunter	Fran. M'Laughlin
Cath. Loughead	John Smiley	Biddy M'Laughlin
Robert Rankin	Henry Dougherty	James Devilt
Manus M'Fadden	Cath. Dougherty	John Blair
Eleanor M'Fadden	Anthy. Dougherty	Allen Kerr
Mathew Nanson	Thomas Stirling	Patrick Browne
Hugh Anderson	Martha Stirling	Bridget Browne
Ann Anderson	Edw. M'Cafferty	Mary Browne
James Anderson	George Blair	Charles M'Kay
Mary Bull	Jane Blair	Wm. Logue
Thomas M'Shane	Catherine Blair	Samuel Boyd
Michael M'Cue	Wm. Blair	Ellen Boyd
Daniel M'Cue	Eliza Blair	Mary Ann Boyd
John Gordon	James Blair	John Gilmour
Robert Hamilton	Hugh Gallen	John Cochran
Andrew Irvine	Mary Gallen	James Kavenagh
John Irvine	Margaret Gallen	Elea. M'Laughlin
Bernard Size	Owen Gallen	Rose Griffeth
Hannah Size	Sally Gallen	Biddy Griffeth
William Moore	Biddy Gallen	Wm. M'Farland
Adam George	Mary Gallen	Mary Logue
John Rea	James Gallen	Biddy Logue
John Young	Catherine	Michael Rodder
Mary Young	John Colvin	Chas. Gallaugher
John Manson	John Hamill	Mary Gallaugher
Wm. Kirkpatrick	Robert Thompson	Cath. Gallaugher
John Kirkpatrick	Roger M'Neal	Patk. Gallaugher
Joseph Steel	Mary Norris	Mich. Gallaugher
Elizabeth Steel	John Coyle	Hugh Gallaugher
Sally Steel	Daniel Coyle	Charles M'Cown
Wm. Knox	James Logue	Bryan Cooney
Samuel Patterson	Thomas Devilt	Samuel Chesnut
Gerard Hunter	James Cullin	John Hanlan
Martha Hunter	Mary Logan	Jame Colvin
John Hunter	Philip M'Gowan	

<u>11-52</u>

(a) Brig Swift, Captain Hitchins, from Dublin, arrived at New York on November 1, 1811 with an unspecified number of passengers.

(b) Mr. Edward Martin died November 2, 1811 at 24 Water st.; had arrived the previous day aboard the Swift. Born in County Kilkenny.

(c) No list published.

<u>11-53</u>

(a) Ship Radius, Captain Pardon Howland, from Londonderry, arrived at New York before November 9, 1811 with an unspecified number of passengers.

(b) Commendation of Captain Howland signed by:

John Montgomery	John Ker
John Crawford	Thomas Beatty
John Dorman	James Roddy
John Galbraith	George Hazleton
Nathan Adams	John Bonar

(c) No list published.

<u>11-54</u>

(a) Ship Erin, from Dublin, arrived at New York before November 16, 1811.

(c) Mr. Thomas and		Thomas Neil	Dublin
Mrs. Robinson	Queen's Co.	James Harrold	"
Mr. Cornelius Smith	Manoch County	David and	
John Lynch	Navan	Dennis Doyle	Dublin
John Androhan	Wexford	Mrs. Cooper	"
William Gibbons	Ohio	Mrs. Riley	Co. Wexford

11-55

(a) Ship Westpoint, Captain T. Holden, from Londonderry, arrived at New York before November 23, 1811.

(c)

Robert Hunter	New York	Joseph M'Coy	
James White	N. L.Vady	and family	Florinscourt
Bernard M'Cosker	Omagh	Catherine Kelley	Fannit
John Henphill		Edward M'Mennomy	Ballybofey
and family	Dugh Bridge	John Kelley	"
John Wawb	Castlefin	John Hilton	Gawagh
David Doak	Fannit	Edward Dogherty	Cauakeel
Susana M'Dermot		Robert Johnston	Pettego
and family	Derry	Francis Johnston	"
Francis Gillespie	Ballyshannon	Alex. M'Alvin	
Daw Griffin	Fannit	and family	Co. Antrim
William Rafferty	Gawagh	Samuel Moorhead	"
Patrick M'Veagh	Campsey	John Jack	"
William Thompson	Carrick	James O'Donnell	Rushey
Robert Henry	Colerain	Ann Donaghey	Roeman
James Martin	N. L. Vady	John Donaghy	Rushey
John Martin	"	Patrick Froster	Straban
Patrick Cartan		George Kirk	Mountcharles
and family	Claudy	George M'Kee	"
Alex. Thompson		James Love	Donagheda
and family	Leuck	Robert Love	"
Alex. Brown		George M'Eliver	"
and family	Aughanwerry	Nancy Wason	Ray
Robert O'Neill		David Hunter	Omagh
and family	Co. Antrim	James C. Sproul	Stranorlar
John Crampsier	Magilligar	Eliza Paul	Omagh
Donaldson Black		John Hunter	N.L.Vady
and family	Co. Tyrone	Farquis M'Gaughrin	Donegall
Elinor M'Cready	Gortward	John Cummings	Ballymoney
Wm. M'Cready	"	Paul Boggs	New York
John Graham	Kilrea	Luke Flyn	Co. Cavan
Thomas Hutchinson	"	John O'Neill	"
Joseph Douglass	"	Ann Masterson	"
Thomas Martin	"	Elizabeth Wardlaw	"
Daw Kelly	Ballintrea	Edward Masterson	"
Ann Coulter	Co. Derry	Elizabeth Hasting	"
Sarah Coulter	"	Edward M'Minimin	Castlefin
Patrick Divin	Ballyshannon	Nancy M'Kagh	"
Hugh Coulter	Pettego	Hugh M'Elwin	Dromore
Hugh Stevenson	Donegal	Hugh Catherwood	Colerain
Mr. Cochran	Ballymoney	Neal Janga	Castlefin

11-56

(a) Ship Hibernia, Captain Graham, from Belfast, arrived at New York before November 30, 1811.

(c)
David M'Clean and family	Ann Blair	Luke Jackson
Mary Willikin and family	H. Stewart	Wm. Thompson
Catherine Coal and family	P. Quin	Mary Reilly
Edward M'Kever and family	Nicholas Lapsy	Margaret Auld
Thomas Mathews and family	John M'Gaw and family	James Getty
Polly Conolly and family	James Leman	Alex. M'Cullough
L. Barklie and family	Margaret Leman	Bernard Doorish
Richard Blair	John M'Neilly	Ann Wright
	James Shepherd	Wm. Freeland
	Robert Peadon	R. Armstrong
	Daniel Quin	James Gaffin
	Hugh Quin	George Roberts
	Wm. Stewart	Thomas Reilly
	Eliz. Armstrong	John Jones
		Benj. Stewart

11-57

(a) Ship Rover, Captain Van Kellock, from Dublin, arrived at New York before November 30, 1811; no mention of passengers.

11-58

(a) Ship Aeolus, Captain Henry, from Newry, arrived at New York before November 30, 1811.

(c)
John Brown and family	George Grady and niece	Lucy Fuller
Robert M'Indov and wife	David Hawthorn and family	John M'Connell
Wm. Burns and family	Wm. Campbell and family	Samuel Evans
John Davidson and family	James Ryers and wife	Alice M'Kenney
Margaret Ferris and family	Henry Holland and family	John Moore
Daniel M'Key and family	Hannah Couden and family	George Black
John George and family	John Trevien and wife	James Kerr
John Class and family	Samuel Kirk and family	Mary Orr
John M'Mullen and family	John Jeffrys and family	Wm. Bell
Robert Cunningham and family	John Murphy	John Bell
	James Harpur	Mary Roark
		Edward M'Quaid
		John Flanigan
		Patrick Flanigan
		Peter Casey
		George Wilkins
		Hugh Crothers

(a) Ship Alexander, Captain Fanning, 47 days from Londonderry, arrived at New York before December 21, 1811.

(c)
James Wright	James Buden	Francis Bradley
and wife	and family	Thomas Swan
William Rea	Alexander Child	Hugh Wallace
and family	Anne M'Clure	Percival Kain
Tully Sleven	Wm. Maitland	John Thompson
and family	John Givun	Dean Knox
Thomas Rogers	Wm. Thompson	Wm. M'Malin
and family	George M'Kinney	Eliza M'Kinney
Francis M'Manus	Robert Moore	Anne Miller
and wife	P. M'Devill	Cath. Bradley
Patrick Campbell	Eliz. Ritchie	Phillip Kelley
and family	Joseph Caldwell	James Collins
		Sally Devlin

11-60

(a) Ship Alknomac, Captain Hicks, departed Sligo on October 3, 1811, passengers landed at Newport, R. I. on December 24, 1811; 79 passengers.

(b) Departed Sligo on October 3. On the night of December 13, the ship ran ashore on Martha's Vinyard. The crew and passengers were saved and remained at Old Town for nine days. Captain Hicks provided a sloop in which the passengers embarked for New York. This sloop was driven ashore on December 24 at Newport, R. I., where the crew and passengers were again landed. The passengers travelled by land to New York in small parties; eight arrived before January 18, 1812, of whom the names of six were published:

Patrick M'Bride	James M'Intire
John O'Rorke	John Rooney
Bartholomew M'Garry	Owen Cammins

(c)
James Henderson	Cath. Kilgallan	Patrick Togher
Edward Smith	James Briarty	Dav. Cunningham
John Smith	Mr. Cassidy's family,	Mary M'Andrew
John Beatty	six in number	Owen Evan
Thomas Kerr	Patrick O'Rorke	John Fletcher
and family	John O'Rorke	Miss Fletcher
Miss Smith	Owen O'Rorke	T. M'Gargle
Patrick Killbride	Mary Roueryni (?)	James Nealis
Owen Finlan	Catherine Tiernan	Mathew Nealis
Bryan O'Rorke	James Wymbs	Patrick Meehan
Darlay Conway	Nelly Teeny	Patrick Harrison
Mrs. Conway	Mrs. Gorman	Patrick Briarty
Bridget Fennigan	Catherine Leyden	John Gallagher
Doby(?) Nealis	Dennis Gorman	John M'Gowran

Bridget Loughlin	Farrell Healy	Thomas Waters
John Parks	Mrs. Healy	Patrick O'Rorke
B. Romayne	James Bremar	Mrs. O'Rorke
Patrick Martin	B. M'Garry	Miss Begley
Mary Romayne	James Clinton	Francis Miller
Bridget Mooney	Thos. M'Gowran	Mrs. Miller
Brian Rooney	Miss M'Gowran	Miss Miller
Paul Rooney	Terry M'Ginley	Terry M'Gargill
John Rooney	James M'Intire	

11-61

(a) Ship Columbia, 45 days from Belfast, arrived at New York before December 21, 1811; went to Amboy with its passengers.

(c) No list published.

11-62

(a) Ship Raleigh, from Dublin, arrived at New York before December 21, 1811.

(b) One seaman was impressed by the British sloop of war Peacock, along with the men marked * below. "The wife of Andrew Mollan, rather than submit to be impiously separated from her husband, followed him on board the British war ship where she now is."

(c) Patrick Bennet	John Rotchford	* Wm. Callahand
and family	Wm. M'Murray	* George Howe
Mary Cranfin	Richard Kench	* Thomas Cosgrave
and family	* Richard Scallan	* Joseph Powell
Thomas English	* John Thompson	* John Johnson
and family	* George Reilly	* Andrew Mollan
Sarah Dander	* Wm. Scofield	

12-1

(a) Ship Joseph and Phoebe, Captain Jack, departed Londonderry around November 15, 1811 bound for New York, stranded at Hempstead, Long Island on January 23, 1812.

(c)

Roger Dougherty	Co. Donegal	Catherine M'Garagher,	Derry
John M'Croghan	"	Fanny M'Garagher	Derry
Nicholas Kerr	Co. Down	Bridget M'Closkey	"
Patrick M'Conaway	Derry	Patrick Fletcher	"
James Fullerton	Donegall	Sally Ann M'Intyre	Donegall
Hugh Wagstaff	Lancaster	Margaret M'Intyre	"
Daniel Coleman	King's Co.	Sally Dougherty	
Michael Larkin	"	and family	Donegall
Patrick M'Donnel	"	Mary Brown	Derry
James Kelley	Tyrone	Elizabeth M'Master	Armagh
John Gultry	Donegall	Margaret Watson	Tyrone
Patrick Collins	Derry	Nancy Anderson	"
John Clarke	Donegall	Eleanor Anderson	"
William Christman	----	Sarah M'Gonan	Derry
Rosina Christman	----	John M'Gonan	"
Francis Loughern			
and family	Tyrone		

12-2

(a) Brig Eliza, Captain Magennis, from Sligo, arrived at Philadelphia on February 15, 1812.

(b) Sailed from Sligo on October 2, 1811; after 28 days was obliged to put into Lisbon for repairs, where she remained four weeks. Off Bermuda, two male passengers were pressed by a British ship of war. The vessel was wrecked near Cape May, New York on February 7, 1812; the crew and passengers were all saved.

(c)

George Gillespy	Co. Derry	Darby Glancey	Co. Sligo
John Gillespy	"	Owen Carrol	"
Mary Gillespy	"	Honora Brannon	"
Ann Gillespy	"	Bridget Gillen	"
Mary Gillespy	"	James Mitchell	"
John Martin	Co. Donegall	---- M'Gillen	"
Robert Martin	"	Thomas Carn	"
Martha Martin	"	Polly Oats	"
William Alligan	"	Ann Lennox	"
Jane White	Co. Sligo	Patrick Conway	"
Margaret White	"	John Hay	"
Ann Moore	"	John Kilfeather	"
William Fair	"	---- Rourke	"
John M'Dermott	"	James Maginnis	"
Hugh M'Dermott	"	Margaret Brannon	"
Peter M'Dermott	"	John Colley	"
Eliza M'Dermott	"	Martin Finn	"
N. Rourke	"	* John Walsh	Co. Mayo
John Moffit	"	* Thomas Team	Co. Westmeath
John Glancey	"	(* passengers pressed)	

12-3

(a) Ship Erin, from Dublin, arrived at New York before April 11, 1812.

(c)
Peter Louergan	Jane Toole	M. --agn--
Ellen O'Keef	Eliza Tool	and family
Cath. Baldwin	Jane Madden	Edward Basey
Sarah Walsh	John Reynolds	Cath. H-li-an
Mary Fagan	Rev. John Ryan	J. M'Cleyen (?)
Edward White	Daniel Cogley	P. M'Cleyen
Edward -romand	Andrew Heekey	Edw. Nugent
James Murphy	James M'Donall	Mary Rae
Patt O'Donnel	John Moore	Thomas Dwyer
G. Bakey	Arch. M'Cartin	George Perceval
Luke Divine	H. Carney	Ellen Wade
	Steph. Kinsela	Patrick Furlong

12-4

(a) Ship Support, from Dublin, arrived at New York before April 11, 1812.

(c)
Mary Keogh	T. Quigley	Michael Leady
G. Richardson	J. Duffy	James Riley
D. Kumely	and family	Garret Bryan
and family	H. Meader	Michael M'Evoy
J. Kittrick	Matt. Murphy	Mary Mackey
and family	Pat Ul-her	Teo. Mansger
T. Ashworth	Mich. Maher	Jacob Calloway
Judith Kehoe	J. Keogh	Joseph Kittrick
J. H. Gordon	and family	

12-5

(a) Ship Protection, Captain Bearns, departed Belfast around February 24, arrived at New York before April 11, 1812.

(c)
R. Hilton	S. and A. Morrison	Hugh Small
J. M. Sinclair	Eliz. Brown	Andrew Dunn
And. Armstrong	Marg. Brown	Mark Sprott
W. Montgomery	Mich. Caralsey	Alex. Laughlin
W. Chamers	J. M'Brier	R. Harcourt
and family	A. Long	and family
G. Hiate	and family	P. Doyle
J. Rainey	James M'Keon	A. Cochran
J. Wallace	Joseph M'Keon	James Mackey
and family	Pt. Glynn	Hugh Caires
W. Black	Edward Carr	James M'Cann
and family	A. Davidson	John Moony
G. Weyman	Johnson Potter	R. Bradford
and family	Saml. Potter	James Hyndman
E. Hughs	Ter. B-onnigan	Joseph M'Cleland
and family	Wm. Bell	John Sweeny
J. and S. M'keon	and family	Arthur Barnes
H. and J. Brown		

12-6

(a) Ship Favourite, from Dublin, arrived at New York before April 11, 1812.

(c)
---- Story and family	Maria Mason
Abm. Hasdy	James Mason
Wm. Caldwell and family	Alex. Stephens
Bridget Keon	Capt. H. G. Hose
Wm. Anderlay	Edward Harvey
Ter. Mechan	Rich. Harvey
John Doyle	T. B. Kettell

12-7

(a) Ship Hibernia, Captain Graham, 23 days from Belfast, arrived in New York before May 2, 1812 with 93 passengers.

(c)
Jno. Allen	J. Wierman	James Harper
and family	and family	William Kelly
Wm. Cole	Jas. M'Given	John Ferguson
Sarah M. Collord	and family	Anne Montgomery
Felin Henry	Jno. M'Keon	Dan. Mollyneux
and family	Adam Crooks	Thos. Ferguson
James Crookes	John Murphy	Bernard O'Neill
William Espy	John Hutchinson	Hugh Kelly
Jno. Graham	Wm. Mitten	John Kelly
Esther Gillespie	James M'Mullan	Robert Kirk
Jno. Carlisle	and wife	James Brady
Wm. Hamilton	Wm. Collins	Eleanor Gallaher
James Watts	Margt. Collins	Alexander Scott
Thos. White	James Clore	Geo. Bodkins
and family	Pat M'Murdy	Wm. Scott
John Bonner	Alex. Humphrey	Robert Wilson
and family	Alex. Kilgent	Thos. Ferguson
		Margt. Clements

12-8

(a) Ship Mary Augusta, departed Londonderry March 29, 1812, arrived at New York before May 2, 1812 with 67 passengers.

(c)

James Garry	Patrick Fodraham	Joseph Swan
James Gallaher	Wm. Lipsett	John M'Comb
David M'Intire	James Gallaher	Jno. Craig
Patrick Monahan	Patrick Gallaher	John Logg
James Warrell	R. Martin	Alexr. Dinsmore
Ann Grant	Mary M'Shee	James Decry
Jno. O'Donnell	Margaret M'Shae	Ann Barton
and family	John Mithas	and family
William M'Clure	Margaret Brien	John M'Kinley
H. Harvey	James M'Cafferty	Edward Grime
Hu M'Keever	and family	John Kenny
Peter Scanlan	Michael Rose	James Kenny
J. Lyon	Owen Garagan	John Martin
Thomas Gr---ks	Daniel Killihan	Bryan M'Taggart
Hanna Nein	Hu Quin	James Stars
Hu Brien	Charles Kelly	David Kenny
Bernard M'Manus	James Seran	James Morrow
Eleanor Brien		

12-9

(a) Ship Triton, Captain Sherry, 38 days from Belfast, arrived at New York before May 2, 1812 with 90 passengers.

(b) Was boarded off Ireland by an English sloop of war and treated politely.

(c) No list published.

12-10

(a) Ship Westpoint, Captain Holden, sailed from Londonderry about March 10, arrived in New York before May 9, 1812.

(c)

John Weir	Andrew Watt	L. M'Manimin
Margt. Siratgrap	Jas. Freeborn	David Galbraith
Patrick Birwin	John Taylor	Jno. Loughry
Mary Irwin	Charles Elder	Micha Loughry
H. Doherty	Saml. Blaney	James Gorman
C. M'Kee	and 6 children	George Patten
Thos. Flemming	Jane Alexander	George Dougherty
Jno. M'Mullen	Henry O'Kean	Mich. M'Gielight
Jas. M'Mullen	M. M'Thilfry	George Casey
Wm. Morre	James Lynch	D. O'Neils
Robt. Byres	Wm. Ferguson	John Ward

Jas. Warten	Robert Patrick	A. Thompson
Robt. Cockblum	Jas. M'Loghlin	Jno. Moan
Charles Smith	Michael Comar	John Derray
Mary Kearney	Thomas Ramsey	Henry Person
John Kernard	Samuel Logan	David King
James Hendrea	M. Carland	Thomas King
R. Dook	Jno. W. Loghland	Ann Sheridan
and wife	Wm. Carland	Wm. Miller
James Travers	Mich. M'Gamage	Samuel Gorrell
H. Doherty	Charles Hurtley	Owen Gorman
Geo. Paschel	Jno. Johneon	Robert Alcorn
James Gowan	Jas. Rupell	Hu M'Felan
Brien Scanlon	Wm. Galliher	and family
Arthur M'Claskey	Hu M'Loghlin	P. Sweeney
Samuel Blair	Mary Mulheris	James Quin
Mathew M'Cully	Jno. Thompson	James Williams

12-11

(a) Ship Radius, Captain Howland, 24 days from Londonderry, arrived at New York before May 9, 1812 with 100 passengers.

(c)

Thomas Brown	Cath. Doherty	Jane Galbraith
Andrew Stewart	and family	John Crotkitt
Jane Rabby	Alexr. Hamilton	Geo. Crotkitt
and family	Jno. Lougherty	James Kerr
J. M'Cormick	Samuel Lynn	James Logan
Andrew Patterson	Wm. Burns	Henry Donnelly
and family	Patrick Mullan	Daniel Denny
	H. Galbraith	Alexander Carson

12-12

(a) Ship Maria Duplex, from Dublin, arrived at New York before May 9, 1812 with six passengers.

(b) April 12, lat. 51, long. 20, the Maria, in a heavy gale of wind from the north, shifted her ballast, water, and provisions, which obligated the crew to cut away the mizen-mast, for the purpose of getting the ship before the wind.

(c)

Patrick Sommers	Co. Carlow	Edward Burns	Co. Monaghan
John Bedlow	"	Patrick Molone	"
John Ryan	"	James Connrig	"

(a) Ship Eliza, Captain Kiddell, from Londonderry, arrived at Philadelphia on May 11, 1812.

(c)

Capt. A. M'Korkell	John M'Laughlin	Jane Gill
Wm. Gallagher	James M'Bea	David M'Carter
Richard M'Mullen	Elizabeth M'Bea	Patrick M'Gowan
Alexan. M'Mullen	Jane M'Bea	James Caldwell
Patrick M'Nulty	Catherine M'Bea	Wm. Summerville
John M'Nulty	Francis M'Bea	John Summerville
Francis Etier	Ann M'Bea	Marg. Summerville
Philip M'Quid	Margaret M'Bea	Andw. Summerville
Hugh M'Nulty	Campbell Johnston	James Summerville
Susanna M'Nulty	James Johnston	Robt. Summerville
Nelly M'Nulty	Wm. M'Colley	Eliza Summerville
Jane M'Nulty	Samuel Edgar	James M'Elven
Mary M'Nulty	Robert Scott	Martha M'Elven
Susanna M'Nulty	Joseph Scott	David Hunter
Peter Lear	Eliza Scott	Wm. Sheriban
Henry Morris	Patrick Scott	William Hog
Rose Morris	Ann Scott	John Rutherford
James Morris	Sarah Scott	David Moore
Dennis Morris	James White	Mary Hunter
Patrick Gormley	Joseph Robb	John M'Nulty
Sarah Walsh	Mary Kingston	John Henderson
Margaret Walsh	Jane Purden	William Ritchie
Rebecca Walsh	Robert Shaw	Nelly Ritchie
Sarah Walsh	Joseph Russel	Margaret Ritchie
Edward Farren	Ester Beck	Jane Ritchie
Mary Farren	Henry Floyd	Sally Ritchie
Ann Farren	Margaret Floyd	Samuel Ritchie
Robert Farren	Jane Lightell	John Ritchie
Patrick M'Bride	Mary Lightell	Henry O'Neill
Owen M'Nulty	Isabella Lightell	Robert George

12-14

(a) Ship Massasoit, Captain Whetten, 28 days from Newry, arrived at New York before May 16, 1812.

(b) Commendation to "Captain Warren" signed by:

Archibald Huston	Dilwerth Brown	Edw. Bloomer
Edward Auston	Theoph. Irwin	George Huston
James Fegan	Henry Yebbs	John Johnston
Robert Ratten	Francis Brown	James Clark
Hugh Dunlap	Thomas Bell	Alex. Brown
Theoph. Lucky	Thos. Donaldson	Jason Roe
James Brown		

(c)

Dilwood Brown, wife and family	nr Ballybay	Patrick Clark	Castleblaney
Jason, Mary, and		Theophilus Leckey	Ballybay
John Roe	nr Ballybay	Sarah Leckey	"
Edward Bloomer	nr Baillboro	Jane Leckey	"
James, Margaret, and		Henry Jebb	"
Alex. Brown	nr Baillboro	Isabella Jebb	"
Robert Houston	"	Theophales Irwen	"
Arm. Houston	"	Sarah Irwen	"
Archibald Houston	"	Thomas Bill	"
Rebecca Houston	"	Thomas Houston	Sharcog
Jane Pepper	Bailboro	Samuel Houston	"
Eliz & Jane Barlow	"	Calvin Sharp	"
Edw. & Jane Houston	"	Francis Donnoly	nr "
Francis Brown	nr Tandregee	George Stewart	"
Peter Brooks	"	James Stewart	"
Richard Johnston	Ballytrane	Michael Fitzsimmons	"
John Johnston	"	James M'Comb	nr Armagh
Betty Johnston	"	Michael Rully	Shascog
Hugh Dunlop, wife and child	Ballytrane	Thomas Donaldson	Armagh
		Henry Kennedy	Lurgan
Elizabeth Brown	"	John Moffitt	Armagh
Thomas Brown	"	George Mason	"
Robert Patter, wife and five children	Armagh	James Fegan and family	Keady
James Clark, wife and child	Castleblaney	Daniel Dosan	"
		James Bill	Ballybay
Bernard Clark	"	John Dougherty	"

57

(a) Bark Edward, Captain Dowdall, sailed from Newry April 11, 1812, arrived at New York on May 16, 1812.

(c)

James Thompson, wife & family	Edward Lappin	James Scott
John Moore	Chas. Holland	Henry Dames
George Young	Felix M'Groeggan	James Sloane
James Young	Pat. Byrne	Felix Cull
John Henry	James M'Nally	Wm. Scott
Catherine Henry	Nancy M'Nally	John Mulhollan
William Robinson	Eliza M'Nally	Wm. Ruddock
Isabella Robinson	Alex. Lewis	Stewart Cooper
John Boyd	John Tomelty	Betty Cooper
Henry Hutchinson	Robert Keith, wife and family	James M'Lory
R. M'Clatchey	John Shannon	Patrick Magee
Wm. M'Kibbin	John Thompson, wife and family	Mary Magee
Patrick Doran	Richard Cox	Margaret Magee
Thomas Cox	Marg. Bailey	John, Lewis, wife and family
Nancy Cox	Joseph Orr	Owen Small
Wm. Anna	Agnes Orr	Kitty Small
James Parker		Wm. Sloan
Hugh Mackey		

12-16

(a) Ship Margaret, Captain Ward, 47 days from Dublin, arrived at New York on May 16, 1812 with an unspecified number of passengers.

(c) No list published.

2-17

(a) Brig Hespa, Captain Boyly, 23 days from Londonderry, arrived at New York before May 30, 1812.

(c)

Felix Donelly	Co. Antrim	Mary Gilmour	Co. Derry
C. Donelly	"	Pat M'Manus	Co. Cavan
M. Cunningham	"	Bryan Gallaher	"
Dan. Purcel		Pat Duan	"
John M'---thine	"	James Willis	Co. Fermanagh
Robert Jones	Co. Donegal	Morgan M'Caffry	"
Fra. Jones	"	Hugh Juda	"
John, James, and		Thomas, Dennis,	
Mary Beaty	"	and Rog. Leonard	"
Wm. Cassidy	"	Mary and	
Arthur and		Biddy Fary	Co. Sligo
Edward Miller	"	Arch. Hicks	Co. Tyrone
Tho. Wm. and		James and	
Elenor Stephensen	"	M. M'Illoy	"
Barney and		Ter. Sarah,	
Peter M'Ginley	"	Francis, Peter,	
John M'Laughlin	"	and Cormic M'Leer	"
Thomas and		Fergus and	
Mary M'Paul	"	Catherine M'Custer	"
Bryen Redden	"	Denis, James,	
Geo. and		Hannah, Hugh,	
Ann Harris	Co. Derry	and Peter M'Mullan	"
Robert Ricky	"	Owen and	
And. Wilson	"	Mary M'Comally	"
David Black	"	Terence M'Quide	"
Arch. Agnes and		Hugh M'Nulty	"
Hannah Campbell	"	Charles Moore	"
Agnes Greeves	"	Geo. Beaty	"
Hugh and		Mich. M'Mullan	"
Cath. Henry	"	John and	
Adam Martin	"	Nathaniel Anderson	"
Mary Campbell	"	John Crossan	"
Robert Bryson	"	Capt. Caldwell	Boston
Jane and			
Eliza Davison	"		

12-18

(a) Brig Mary, Captain Boggs, from Coleraine, arrived at New York before June 20, 1812.

(c)
George Hazleton	Matthew Elder	John Thompson
George Martin	Hanry Willis	Robert Law
Michael Dogherty	James M'Kindry	John O'Neill
Thomas Stewart	James Johnson	James M'Laughlin
John Whiteford	James Patterson	Catherine Armstron
Thomas Dickson	Mary Patterson	Joseph Wier
Margaret Houston	John Patterson	Alexander Scott
Margaret Houston	John Pattison	William Cristie
Samuel M'Laughlin	John Reid	Thomas Burns
James M'Laughlin	Robert M'Afee	James Wilson
Robert Gilland	Henry Doherty	Thomas Mitchell
Alexander Adams	John Reynold	James Mitchell
John Stewart	Hugh M'Colgan	John Mitchell
James Kirkpatrick	Robt. Stewart	Margaret Mitchell
Margaret Kirkpatrick	and family	John M'Ilereavy
Jane Kirkpatrick	Esther Armstrong	and family

12-19

(a) Ship Alexander, Captain Burns, from Londonderry, arrived at New York before June 20, 1812.

(c)
Miss Clotilda Elliott, Leitrim		Mary Aiken	Donegal
John M'Kim	Derry	Robert Corbit	"
Michael Allen	"	Samuel M'Intire	"
James W. Patterson	New York	Sarah M'Intire	"
Owen Durish	Fermanagh	Richard Beaty	"
Catherine Durish	"	Anne Beatty	"
Arthur Graham	"	Archibald Long	"
Bridget Graham	"	Mary Long	"
Peter Breen	"	William Barr	"
Owen Murray	"	Eleanor Barr	"
William Kerr	"	John Barr	"
James M'Gir	"	Michael Doherty	"
John Graham	"	Mary Doherty	"
Eliza Graham	"	William Doherty	"
Samuel Osborne, sen.,	Dublin	Bryrn Quigley	"
Samuel Osborne, jun.,	"	John Durne	"
Mary M'Fadden	Donegal	Alexander Brown	"
Nancy M'Fadden	"	Rebecca Brown	"
Dominick Coll	"	Isabella Brown	"
Bryan Roper	"	Roger Doherty	"
Peggy Roper	"	Emma Doherty	"
Archibald Aiken	"	William Henry	"
Sarah Aiken	"	Joshua Smullen	"
Eliza Aiken	"	Sarah Smullen	"

Arther Mehain	Donegal	George Kerr	Tyrone
Mary M'Ilwain	"	Catherine Kerr	"
James M'Culloch	Tyrone	James Kerr	"
Betty M'Culloch	"	George Kerr	"
Margaret M'Culloch	"	Joseph Kerr	"
Mary M'Culloch	"	William Kerr	"
Thomas M'Culloch	"	Ellen Kerr	"
John Irwine	"	Richard Kerr	"
Mary Irwine	"	Richard Bloomfield	"
William Woods	"	William Stevenson	"
Mary Woods	"	James Brown	"
Nelson Woods	"	John Brown	"
Thomas Woods	"	James Ferrall	"
John Eilis	"	Henry Connor	"
Anne Chambers	"	Daniel Boyle	"
George Scott	"	Francis Gallaher	"
Eliza Scott	"	Mary McGinness	"
Anthony Woods	"	Stewart McGinness	"
Daniel Doherty	"		

The following passengers by the above vessel, were pressed by the British frigate Morgiana, in lat. 41 40, long. 57 25.

Hugh O'Brien	Fermanagh	Edward Doherty	Donegall
Teague M'Feaden	Donegall	Brian Hapan	Derry
Samuel Corbett	"	Peter Hoan	Donegall
James Cresholm	Tyrne	Mich. M'Cormick	"
Peter Kelly	Donegall	Wm. Stevenson	Tyrone
James Williams	"	Robert Stevenson	"
John Druimmend	Fermanagh	Pat. M'Collum	Derry
Pat. Curry	"	Wm. Ward	Tyrone
Saml. M'Intire	Derry	John Ward	"
Robert Fletcher	Leitrim	Manus Connor	"
Daniel Rouso	"	Hugh Dougherty	Donegall
John Begley	Tyrone	Brian Quigley	"
Martin Beil	Donegall	Pat M'Guire	Fermanagh
Con Finn	"	John Bresland	Donegall
John Wilson	Fermanagh	Manus M'Fadden	"

12-20 to 12-25

The following six vessels arrived at New York before June 20, 1812. No
mention of passengers was made and no lists were published. Included with
these were the Alexander (12-19) and the Mary (12-18), similarly lacking
mention of passengers, but for which lists were published. The Aeolus and
the Perseverance had each carried passengers to America in 1811.

12-20: The Augusta, Captain Hathaway, from Londonderry.
12-21: The Aeolus, Captain Henry, from Newry.
12-22: The Perseverance, Captain Inkhim, from Dublin.
12-23: The Standard, Captain Holms, from Newry.
12-24: The Enterprise, Captain Hinman, from Newry.
12-25: The Susanah, Captain Bunce, from Londonderry.

12-26

(a) Brig Pleiades, Captain Backus, from Belfast, arrived at New York before
June 20, 1812.

(b) On June 13 the Pleiades was reported captured by His Majesty's brig
Colibri and taken into Halifax. It was presumed in New York that the
passengers would be transported to the island of St. John's. When the
ship arrived in New York, no mention of passengers was made.

(c) No list published.

12-27

(a) Ship Rising States, Captain Stillwell, from Newry, arrived at Philadelphia
on June 17, 1812.

(c) William Brown   John H. Hanley   Th. M'Caffery
    Jane Brown   Felix M'Muldoon   John Boyd
    Mathew Watson   Robert Gill   Elizabeth Boyd
    Isabella Watson   Thomas Gill   Elizabeth Boyd
    Andrew Watson   Michael M'Crane   Samuel Boyd
    James Watson   Patrick Cassidy   Rosannah Boyd
    Mathew Watson junr. Patrick Vallely   William Boyd
    Mary Watson   Bridget Vallely   Jane Young
    Sarah Watson   Francis Hughes   James Crawford
    John Black   David M'Waters   Samuel M'Dowell
    Henry Gorman   John Hagan   Mary J. Dickson
    James Gorman   Jane Hagan   Benjamin Dickson
    William Ligget   Isaac Hagan   Andrew Hood
    James M'Caskey   Ann Jane Hagan   Joseph Mulholland
    Thomas Eager   Elizabeth Moffett   Francis Hughes
    Charles Leonard   Martha Moffett   Alexander Henry

James Ray	Francis Breen	William M'Anary
John Ray	Thomas Mullan	Gabriel Cathcart
William Barnes	Bridget Mullan	Cor. M'Avenny
Peter Hughes	James M'Dougall	Cath. M'Avenny
Ann Hughes	Edward Murphy	John M'Avenny
Thomas Hughes	Robert Bleakly	Michael Watt
Bernard Hughes	Samuel Stewart	

12-28

(a) Brig Retrieve, Captain Hunt, from Londonderry, arrived at Philadelphia on June 23, 1812.

(b) Was reported under detention at Londonderry on January 29. Was boarded off the capes of the Delaware by the British frigate Belvidere and fifteen passengers were pressed.

(c)

William Reynolds	Ballymony	Henry M'Namara	Augher
Agnes Reynolds	"	John Boak	Strabane
Nancy M'Gerry	"	Letitia Boak	"
Alexander Robeson	Raphoe	James Robinson	Londonderry
Rebecca Robeson	"	Thomas Collingwood	"
James Robeson	"	Jane Collingwood	"
John Robeson	"	James Richard	Ballymoney
Margaret Robeson	"	Nancy Richard	"
Wm. Robeson	"	Jane Richard	"
Moses Speer	"	William Richard	"
Mary Lawson	Stewartstown	Elizabeth Richard	"
Joseph Lawson	"	Jane Richard	"
Agnes Lawson	"	John M'Calden	Clones
Isabella Lawson	"	Margaret M'Calden	"
Thomas Lawson	"	William M'Calden	"
Hugh Lawson	"	John M'Calden	"
Margaret Lawson	"	John Hamilton	Newton Limavady
Margaret Lawson	"	Samuel Hamilton	"
Mary Lawson	"	Thomas Steel	"
Sarah Lawson	"	Daniel Quinn	Stewartstown
Susan Mulvenna	"	William Caldwell	Drumcroon
Owen Donnelly	Augher	Sarah Kerr	Raphoe
Catherine Donnelly	"	John Dougherty	Londonderry
Hugh Donnelly	"	Rose Dougherty	"
Patrick Donnelly	"	James Ellis	Strathane
Ann Donnelly	"	Mary M'Crea	"
James Donnelly	"	John M'Crea	"
Neil Donnelly	"	Letitia M'Crea	"
David Donnelly	"	Elizabeth M'Crea	"
Robert Johnston	"	Neil M'Coy	Newton Limavady
Sally Johnston	"	Thomas Ellis	Newton Stewart
Thomas Johnston	"	Neil Divine	Strathane
Sally Johnston	"	Alfred Loughery	Philadelphia

<u>12-28</u> (c), continued

    Impressed Passengers:

John M'Coy	Strathane	John Henry	Ballymony
Samuel Young	Stewartstown	John Doherty	Newton L'vady
James Speer	"	David Laughlin	"
Arther M'Neil	Augher	Thomas Clark	"
David Thompson	Stewartstown	Francis Robinson	Raphoe
David Gallbraith	Raphoe	Samuel Robinson	Strabane
James M'Daid	Londonderry	Alexander Lemen	Newton Stuart

<u>12-29</u>

(a) Brig Pallas, Captain Cole, from Lough Swilly, arrived at Philadelphia
on July 2, 1812.

(b) Reported under detention at Lough Swilly on January 29.

(c) John Kelley	Culdaff	Peter Jones	Jones Town
Mary Kelley	"	James Jones	"
Patrick Kelley	"	William Hamilton	Tyrone
John M'Laughlin	Catridge	Jane Hamilton	"
Henery M'Laughlin	"	William Hamilton	"
James Gibson	Ballymalland	John Hamilton	"
Jane Gibson	"	Mary Hamilton	"
Thomas Gibson	"	Joseph Hamilton	"
Andrew Shepherd	Fermanagh	Peter Hamilton	"
Elizabeth Shepherd	"	Betsey Hamilton	"
Thomas Shepherd	"	Denis Hamilton	"
James Shepherd	"	Arthur Graham	Cloonish
William Shepherd	"	Elizabeth Graham	"
Margaret Shepherd	"	William Graham	"
Jane Shepherd	"	Thomas Graham	"
Maurice Shepherd	"	Gabriel Moor	Kelty Glas (?)
Philip Shepherd	"	William Foster	Clandehork
Thomas Elliot	Frillick (?)	Martha Foster	"
William Elliot	"	William M'Bride	"
John Mathews	Donemanna	George M'Caskey	"
William Mathews	"	Martha M'Caskey	"
Margaret Mathews	"	Charles Aigue (?)	"
Alexander Rankin	Ballyeronan	John M'Closky	Kilrea
John Rankin	"	Martha M'Closky	"
James Rankin	"	Patrick M'Closky	"
Elizabeth Rankin	"	* James M'Ginley	
John Johnston	Drumnacross	* Thomas Orr	
Denis Bradely	Magillegan	* Owen Leonard	

                                      * Impressed

(a) Ship Mary, Captain Wallington, from Londonderry, arrived at Philadelphia on July 8, 1812.

(b) While at Moville Bay awaiting customs clearance, the Mary, the Bristol, and two other American vessels were boarded by the crew of His Majesty's schooner Barbara under Lt. Morgan. Crewmen and passengers were seized and all were very roughly treated. The people of Londonderry were appalled at this action, but they blamed the commanding officer, not their own government.

(c)

Name	Place	Name	Place
Darley Sloan	Irvinstown	Mary Ellis	Londonderry
John Glenn	Coleraine	William Ellis	"
Richard M'Lean	"	Robert Ellis	"
John Park	"	Catherine Kerr	"
Elizabeth Park	"	Robert Culbert	Larne
David Park	"	Margery Warkman	"
Nancy Park	"	John M'Devitt	Strabane
Betty Park	"	Mary M'Devitt	"
William Park	"	Margaret Ralston	"
Peter Park	"	Martha Ralston	"
Denis Karney	Carn	William Ralston	"
Daniel Karney	"	Joseph Ralston	"
Edward Karney	"	Elizabeth Cotterson	Strabane
Roger Karney	"	James Cotterson	"
Daniel Karney	"	Nancy Cotterson	"
Unity Karney	"	Lawrence M'Kee	Lisburn
Mary M'Laughlin	"	Ellen M'Kee	"
Owen Dougherty	"	Rose Kelly	Strabane
John Smith	"	Eleanor Kelly	"
Jane Smith	"	Andrew Hamilton	N. Stewart
Eliza Smith	"	Ann Stewart	Dungiven
Edward Harold	"	John Howard	Londonderry
Owen Dougherty	"	Nancy Kearns	Strabane
Ann Dougherty	"	Elizabeth King	Clones
Grace Gillen	"	Ann King	"
Charles Christy	"	John Kerr	Castlefin
Charles M'Laughlin	Buncrana	Elizabeth Rose	"
William M'Daid	"	Henery M'Kee	Maghera
Eleanor M'Laughlin	"	Jane M'Kee	"
John Doherty	"	Grace M'Cready	Dungiven
Felix M'Cleery	Tintona	Ann Carrigan	Londonderry
Rose M'Cleery	"	John Carrigan	"
Patrick M'Cleery	"	Robert Loughead	Dunfanaghy
Hugh M'Cleery	"	Thomas Ellis	Raphoe
Ann M'Cleery	"		
Patrick Smith	"		
Elizabeth Cassidy	"		

<u>12-30</u> (c), continued.

Impressed Passengers:

James Park	Coleraine	Owen M'Laughlin	Buncrana
James Russel	"	Henery M'Laughlin	"
David Wilson	"	Peter Doherty	"
John Kearney	Carn	James Sproul	Strabane
Daniel Kearney	Carn	Patrick M'Arann	Irvingstown
Owen M'Laughlin	"	William Dougherty	N. Stewart
John M'Laughlin	"	John Mayberry	Gawagh
Patrick M'Fall	"	James M'Cready	Dungiven
Edward Reddy	"	Mathew Boogs	Ballyhofey
Edward Doherty	"	David Laird	"
Bryan Doherty	"	James Smyth	Dunnomanagh
Edward M'Ginnis	"	James Thompson	Ballymoney
John Kearney	"	Thomas Burt	Glenavey

<u>12-31</u>

(a) Ship Bristol, Captain Barker, from Londonderry, arrived at New York before July 18, 1812.

(b) See 12-30.

(c)
Denis M'Bride	Jane M'Clay	John Fulton
John Chambers and family	John Scanlin	Eliza Fulton jun.
James Wallace	Mary Scanlin	Isabella Fulton
Mary Wallace	William Murray	James Memna
Mary Wallace jun.	Roger Sweeney	Allen Tosh
Jane Wallace	Francis Conway	Wm. Gordon
Bryan M'Turner	Thomas Kinkede	and family
Cath. M'Turner	Wm. Gallagher	John Dempsey
Ann M'Turner	Eliza Gallagher	Nelly Dougherty
Philip Sweeny	James Gallagher	Mich. M'Gillan
Arthur Durnen	Margaret Fulton	Denis Dougherty
And. M'Farlan and family	David Fulton	Mary Dougherty
Micl. Gillespy and family	Ann Fulton	and child
Adam M'Clay	James Walker	Wm. Ferguson
And. M'Clay & family	Eliza Fulton	James M'Cormick
	John Fulton	Rose M'Cormick
	Isabella Fulton	Darley Conaghty
	Andrew Fulton	

(a) Ship Venus, departed Londonderry around May 10, arrived at New York before July 18, 1812.

(c)

Jonathan Purse	John Henderson	James Mackey
Money Purse	and family	Sarah Mackey
Jonathan Purse	Hugh Doherty	Chales Mulhattan
and family	and family	Patrick Boyle
James Gulmour	James Mulhattan	Jos. Stevenson
and family	Hugh Carney	and family
John Graham	Arch Vertu	James M'Can
Mary Graham	Michal Vertu	Money M'Can
Henry Bossman	John Jeffers	John M'Can
Matthew Bossman	Patrick Harkin	Wm. M'Laughlin
Elizabeth Ross	James Larn	James Irwin
Jane Ross	James Henry	Elizabeth Irwin
Biddy M'Gurk	Edward M'Colgan	Nilly M'Laughlin
Jane M'Natuig	James Monaghan	Samuel Patterson
Cathin Lithgou	James Dougherty	Cath. Lagee
Nany Lithgou	Edward M'Dead	and child
John Clemmons	Daniel Sweeny	Robert Adams
Mary Clemmons	James Wilson	Robert Carey
Eliza Clemmons	Thos. Hamilton	James Carey
Robt. Kennedy	and family	John M'Colgan
and family		

12-33

(a) Ship Atlas, from Belfast, arrived at New York before July 18, 1812.

(c)

John Marshal	James Conery	James M'Gurney
and family	Peter M'Eldowney	and family
Hu M'Vea	Donald M'Kennen	John Murray
John Hillon	John M'Williams	Francis Dwlin
John Steel	and family	and family
Henry School	John Bradley	Arch. Clendenning
Mich. M'Calluch	Nancy Bradley	and family
and family	Anthony Conway	John Grieve
John M'Alester	Charles Herron	James Wilson
and family	and family	Robert Brown
John Campbell	Dominick M'Elvea	Robert Robinson
Mich. Davis	Francis Kelly	and family
and family	John Hamilton	

12-34

(a) The Felix, Captain Cornwall, from Galway, arrived at New York before
August 1, 1812.

(c) All passengers were from Galway.

Hugh Cawfield	John Mitchell & wife	John Fleming
and family	Martin M'Guire	and wife
Nancy Murray	Bryan Lammin	Mrs. Dorsey
Wm. Hogg	Bartlis O'Donnell	Miss M'Lean
and wife	Mark Vowser	Mr. Hansbrow
Patrick Byrne	Thomas M'Dermot	Mrs. Hatch
Daniel Cochlin	Mrs. Coleman	Mrs. Walsh
John Turey	and three children	

12-35

(a) Ship Ontario, Captain Campbell, from Newry, arrived at New York before
August 15, 1812 with passengers.

(b) "June 14 off the island of Roughry NW coast of Ireland was boarded by
the British frigate Fortuna and treated politely."

(c) No list published.

12-36

(a) Ship North Star, Captain Peterson, from Londonderry bound for New York
with passengers, arrived at Bath before August 15, 1812.

(c) No list published.

12-37

(a) Ship Bellisarius, Captain Morgan, bound from Belfast to Boston with 52
passengers.

(b) Reported captured on August 10, 1812 to the west of the Grand Bank by the
British sloop of war Morgiana under Captain Scott. The passengers were
removed and the Bellisarius was sent to the U.S. carrying the crews of
several captured American vessels.

(c) No list published.

12-38

(a) Brig Prudence, Captain Anderson, bound from Dublin to New York with passengers.

(b) Captured on August 10, 1812 by the Morgiana and sent to Halifax with her passengers. The home port of the Prudence was Charleston.

(c) Mr. George Puffer of New York, with his wife and children, was aboard. No complete list was published.

12-39

(a) Brig Narind, Captain James Stewart, from Newry, arrived at New York on August 14, 1812.

(c)

---- Brennan	Tenderagee	Elizabeth Lockhart	
Margaret Brennan	"	and family	Castleblaney
Thomas Monaghan		James White	
and family	Tenderagee	and family	Castleshone
Thomas Reed	Richell	William Slone	
Alex Irwin	Aughnacloy	and family	Rathfriland
Jno. Patterson		Samuel Moore	"
and wife	Castleshane	Pat. Hagan	
Arthur Patterson	"	and wife	Dunganon
Jane Patterson	"	Bernard Brennan	Castleshone
James Murphy	Castleblaney	Ann Robinson	"
Robert Farley	"	Samuel Gillespie	
Pat. Trainor	Newry	and family	Ardaghy
Wm. Dellaney	Bambridge	Pat. Kelly	Monaghan
John Dellaney	"	John Kelly	"
Hugh Coin	Armagh	Thos. Wood	"
Robert Wilson	"	Wm. Fauls & wife	H-nedy
John Moore	"	Miss Welsh	Dungannon
Wm. Knox		And. Caldwell	
and wife	Rathfriland	and wife	Rathfriland
Ruth Best		Thomas Crusley	"
and family	Gilford	John Quin	Keady
Elizabeth M'Goffin	"	George Mills	New York

12-40

(a) Schooner Eunice, Captain John Peters, from Londonderry, arrived at New
York on August 14, 1812.

(c)
Ann Clark		John M'Gee	Taboyne
and family	Dunbar	Hugh Nelis	"
Henry Dougherty	Glensooly	Joseph Finniston	Toombridge
David Taylor		Ann Finniston	"
and family	Moeheelon	Patrick Gallaugher	Mountgaulin
John Guthry		Margaret Magee	Rapho
and family	Drumschool	Catherine Magee	"
Biddy Rice	Ballybay	James Kyle	Brakey
Mary Kane	Ballycastle	William Snodgrass	Colraine
John Kean	"	John M'Clelland	Carnamay
Patrick Dougherty	Glensooly	Thomas Kirkwood	Ballymoney
Margaret Chambers	Taboyne	Thomas Kirkwood jr.	"
Nancy M'Gowan	"	Andrew Bratton	Drumschool
Sarah M'Gowan	"		

70

__13-1__

(a) Cartel brig Catherine Ray, Captain Hicks, from Liverpool, arrived at
New York before May 29, 1813.

(c)

Edward Campbell	London	Jane Atkinson	
John Richardson	Liverpool	and 3 children	Ireland
Robert Wilson	Virginia	Mrs. C.P.F. O'Hara	
David Bruce	New York	and 4 children	Ireland
Nathaniel Macy	"	Mary Kenny	"
John Dodd	Albany	Letitia M'Kinley	"
Mary Jordan		John M'Kinley	"
and family	Ireland		

15-1

(a) Brig Nautilus, Captain Atkins, from Dublin, arrived at New York before September 2, 1815.

(c)
John Lear	Dublin	Daniel Stinton	City of Limerick
Patrick Walsh	"	John Moiris	Boyle, Co. Roscom
John Cavanaugh	"	James Donohoo	Co. Meath
Michael M'Cullagh	"	Luke Fay	Navan
John Murphy	"	Fras. Reilly	Granard
Wm. George Daly	Cavan	---- Shales	Shercock, Co. Ca•
Michael Reilly	"	---- Reilly	"
Chr. Ivory,		Robert Johnson	Wicklow
wife & child	Co. Limerick		

15-2

(a) Ship Amphion, Captain Jones, from Dublin, arrived at New York before September 2, 1815.

(c)
Rev. Michael Carroll	City of Kilkenny	Francis Malone	Killesandra
Peter Bannan	Drogheda	William Patterson	King's Court, Co.
Thomas Delahunt	"	Charles Clark	" Cavan
Miss Farrell	"	Bryan Lynch	"
John Kelly	Dublin	John Reilly	"
Thomas Purdon	"	Joseph Patterson	Co. Cavan
Patrick Kearns	"	Thos. Smith	
Edward Deroy	"	and wife	Co. Cavan
James Deroy	"	Nich Fegan	
Hugh Kelly	Bainbridge	and wife	Castle Pollard
Mr. Murtagh		John Byrne	Co. Tipperary
and wife	Co. Longford	Nicholas Caffry	"
Francis Deale	Granard	James Behan	"
Hugh Masterson	"	Lawrence Walsh	"
Hugh Kelly	Cavan	Hugh Walsh	"
Margaret Kelly	"	James Arnold	" (Clogheen)
Thomas Smith jun.	"	Martin Cogly	Wexford
Bernard Smith	"	James Clinch	Bailiborough
John M'Cabe	"	Mrs. Rowland	
Michael M'Manus	Killesandra	and child	----
Patrick Brady	"	Nicholas Whelan	----
James Hewett	"	James Byrne	----
Thomas Sherdon	"	Edward Barry	----
Jane Sherdon	"	John Smith	England

(a) Brig Helen, Captain Fitzgerald, from Sligo, arrived at New York before
September 2, 1815.

(c)
John Stephens	Thomas Connolan	Charles Ferguson
Thomas Martin	Andrew Gamel	Patrick Molloy
George Kerr	Mary McDugal	Daniel Mason
Bernard O'Rorke	George Lindsay	Darby Gillan
Winifred Waters	Patrick O'Rorke	Sally Gillan
Hugh Conway	Henry Dalton	James Cassady
William Henderson	William Wilkinson	Thomas Faley
Pat. Golrick Martin	John Wilkinson	Robert Lindsay
John Golrick Martin	Owen McLean	Richard Lindsay
Patrick McManus	Bridget McLean	Patrick Callaghan
Maurice Brady	Michael O'Beirn	Mr. Thompson
Terence Golrick	Michael Crossan	John McDougal
B. McCormack	Thomas Costello	

15-4

(a) Ship Virginia, Captain Jonathan Hillman, from Waterford, arrived at New
York on September 2, 1815.

(c)
John Percival	Waterford	Catherine Tobin	Waterford
Henry Godkin	"	Maurice Power	"
Henry Johnson	"	Bridget Hayden	"
Martha Johnson (child)	"	Bridget Hayden jun.	"
Sarah Johnson	"	Richard Clark	
Anthony Daly	"	and wife	"
Andrew Spratt	"	George Johnson	"
Stephen Blanchfield	"	Jas. Mahony	Wexford, a
Patrick Whelan	"	citizen of the U.S.	
John Morgan	"	Henry Gowan	Waterford
Francis Grace	"	Peter Wells	"
James Coughlan	"	Anthony Jeffers	"
Daniel Flood	"	John Whit	"
John Recard		Thomas Godfrey	"
and wife	"	Thomas Egan	"
Wm. O'Donnell		Michael Dooling	"
and wife	"	Peter Connelly	"

15-5

(a) Brig Christopher, Captain N. Ingraham, from Belfast, arrived at New York on September 2, 1815.

(c)
John Ellison, printer	Belfast	Obediah Murdoch	Co. Down
Alexander M'Kay	Co. Antrim	John Crany	"
James M'Gowan	"	a citizen of the U.S.	
Daniel Linn	"	John Ferguson	Co. Down
William Braith	"	Tho. Cumming, carpenter	"
Hugh Jameson	"	Hans Cumming	"
Henry Gillen	"	Rose M'Carty	Co. Armagh
Robert M'Kee		John Clark	"
and wife	"	Sam. M'Cleary,	
James Wilson	"	blacksmith	Co. Tyrone
David Patterson	"	Michael Fingusin	"
John Campbell	"	Eliza Duff	"
William Steel, clerk	"	Daniel McCann	Derry
George Dale, carpenter	"	Charles O'Neil,	
James M'Bride, "	"	shoemaker	Derry
Alexander M'Mullen	"	Samuel Flood	"
William Walkinshaw	"	Thos. Scellan, clerk	Dublin
Edward M'Carden	Co. Down	William Mullay	"
Quinton Shannon	"	Daniel Carmichael	New York
Thomas Herrin	"	Thomas Webster	England

15-6

(a) Schooner Mary, Captain Paul Burrows jr., from Dublin, arrived at New York on September 23, 1815.

(c)
Thomas Finegan	Thomas Mulvany	John Kemple
Samuel Clebborn	Mark Ennis	James Moran
Peter Henney	Henry Malone	William Tracey
David R. Blood	Margaret Cross	Michael M'Daniel
Miss Ann O'Connell	Peter Smith	Mary M'Daniel
Jeremiah Conner	Charles McGovern	Mary M'Arnon
James Gafney	Michael Muldawney	Mary M'Arnon (child
James Brady	Thomas Killen	

15-7

(a) Brig Mary, from Dublin, landed at Newport before October 7, 1815.

(b) Bound for New York, but encountered a severe gale off of Long Island which compelled her to put into Newport. She carried 77 passengers.

(c) No list published.

(a) Ship George, Captain Craig, 56 days from Belfast, arrived at New York on October 14, 1815.

(c)

John Charters	Antrim	James Irvine	Markethill
Samuel M'Gouran	Comber	Joseph Smith	Drimoragh
Washington Dawson	Belfast	Hugh Latham	Crumlin
William Henry	"	George Bell	Castlereagh
William Everitt	"	Hugh Shannon	
Samuel Hill	Ballycastle	and wife	Belfast
Arthur Gardner	Belfast	Hugh Garrett	Saintfield
Elizabeth Gardner	"	Thomas Semple	Aghadowy
Eleanor Gardner	"	James M'Atier	"
Deborah Gardner	"	James Dobson	Moy
Elizabeth Gardner	"	Susan Dobson	" /
Arthur Gardner jun.	"	John Dobson	"
Hugh Boden	Ballykeel	William Dobson	"
Margaret Frazer	Belfast	Mary Dobson	"
Sarah Frazer	"	Fanny Dobson	"
John Frazer	"	Mary Cullen	"
Eliza Frazer	"	John Lee	"
Jane Frazer	"	Thomas Lee	"
Joseph Frazer	"	Simon Lee	"
John Mullan	Aughdowy	George Lee	"
Cicely Mullan	"	Sarah Lee	"
William Mullan	"	Eleanor Hice	Drumgolen
Arthur Mullan	"	Hugh Armstrong	"
John Dempsey	"	Daved Sampson	Dundee
John Miller	Randlestown	Thomas Mathews	"
Andrew Douglass	Belfast	Andrew Thompson	New York
William Irvine	Markethill	Samuel Harbison	Philadelphia

(a) Ship James Bailey, from Belfast, arrived at New York on October 26, 1815.

(b) A son, her first child, was born to Mrs. "Blakely" on the morning of October 23, while the ship was off Sandy Hook.

(c)

Richard Cochran	Grange	Ruth Woods	Rich-Hill
Mary Ann Cochran	"	William Martin	Aughill
* Jane Cochran	"	Martha Martin	"
* Agnes Cochran	"	* Rachel Martin	"
* Isaac Cochran	"	William Gray	Edinburg
John Hagan	Co. Tyrone	Roger M'Ralin	Ballymena
Samuel Duff	"	William M'Clellon	"
William Watson	"	James Reid	"
John Shaw	Co. Antrim	Patrick Johnston	"
David Dickson	Co. Derry	John Marshall	Co. Antrim
Peter M'Lean	"	Margaret Marshall	"
Robert Spencer	Co. Antrim	* Samuel Marshall	"
King M'Ilrath	"	* Isabella Marshall	"
James Rainey	Ballymena	* Mary Marshall	"
Abraham Smith	Co. Antrim	William Blame	Ballymena
Hugh Smith	"	Hugh Corry	Cookstown
John Low	"	Andrew Jameson	Grey Abbey
Deekey Agnew	Ballynase	Daniel Doherty	Belfast
William Crawford	Belfast	Catherine Doherty	"
Thomas Thompson	Dromore	Mary Doherty	"
Alexander M'Cambridge	Cushendern	Mr. M'Clelland	Co. Down
Mary Thompson	Dromore	Mrs. M'Clelland	"
John Anderson	Coleraine	* Mary M'Clelland	"
Mrs. Anderson	"	Edward Lee	Co. Cavan
* A. Anderson	"	Jane Lee	"
Thomas Carlin	Co. Down	* Alexander Lee	"
William Woods	Richhill	* Anne Lee	"
Mary Harris	"	* Mary Lee	"
James M'Clelland	"	Joseph Robinson	"
Samuel M'Clelland	"	James M'Curdy	Coleraine
Patrick Keanen	"	Jane M'Curdy	"
William Bleakley	Drumbo	* Wm. M'Curdy	"
John Bleakley	"	Robert Kerr	Ballymena
Jane Bleakley	"	Mrs. Letitia Stewart	Belfast
Charles Stewart	Rushmills	* Rebecca Stewart	"
John Stewart	"	* Alexander Stewart	"
James Neil	Ballymoney	William Robin	Banbridge
Margaret Neil	"	---- Foster	Belfast
John Stewart	Rushmills	George Forsyth	Magherafelt
Sally Stewart	"	William Duncan	"
Rose Stewart	"	John M'Naughton	Monaghan
Robert Longman	"	John Maxwell	Rushmills
William Deymour	Drumbo	Mrs. T. Maxwell	"
David Shannon	"	* Margaret Maxwell	"
John Brown	Dennyroign	* Eliza Maxwell	"
James Spark	Derrock	James Stewart	"
James Brown	Aughnacloy	Joseph Painter, surgeon, Magherafelt	
John Campbell	Co. Antrim	William Davidson	Ballybanden
John Quin	Cookstown	John Robinson	Newtownards

* children

76

(a) Ship George and Albert, 47 days from Dublin, arrived at Philadelphia on October 23, 1815.

(c)
William Campbell	Michael Smith	Peter Sheppard
Thomas Spunner	Philip Reily	and wife
James R. Keown	Thomas Brown	Charles March
Edward Conner	Thomas M'Casle	Thomas West
John Conner	John Boyle, wife	Murtoch Geoghegan
Patrick Peppard	and three children	Henry Geoghegan
and wife	John Cunningham	Isaac Russel
Robert Coleman,	Laurence Nugent	Patrick Brady
wife & child	James M'Sheldon	Robert Lea
Thomas Wilson	Francis M'Kay	William Kennedy
William M'Cann	Charles Weeks	Edward Kennedy
Thomas Fitzgerald	James Sheppard	John Birk
Phillip Smith	and wife	

15-11

(a) Brig Maria, from Dublin, arrived at New York on November 5, 1815, via Newport, R.I.

(c) Margaret Abbott and family, England
George David, Scotland

15-12

(a) Brig Charles, Captain Fawcett, 74 days from Dublin, arrived at New York on November 10, 1815.

(c)
James Madden	Kilkenny	* William Latham	Dublin
A. Butterworth	Naas	John Murphy	"
John Hart	Dublin	J. Elliot	"
John Ploughman	"	Henry Jones	
John Gowran	"	John Moore	Co. Carlow
Miss Kelly	"	Richard Farrell	Co. Meath
Thomas Latham		Patrick Reilly	Co. Longford
and wife	Dublin	Thomas King	Balbriggan
Henry Latham	"	Edward M'Kernan	Co. Leitrim
Martha Latham	"	Patrick M'Kernan	"
* Nathaniel Latham	"	John Foster	Co. Tyrone
* Elias Latham	"	* children	

15-13

(a) Brig Two Friends, from Halifax, Nova Scotia, arrived at New York on November 13, 1815.

(c) James M'Carter   Ireland
    Mrs. Robinson and family   Ireland

15-14

(a) Ship William, from Liverpool, arrived at New York on November 14, 1815.

(c) James O'Leary   Dublin
    Alexander D. Ewing   Londonderry

15-15

(a) Ship Mexico, from Liverpool, arrived at New York on November 14, 1815.

(c) Henry Maguire   Dublin   Margaret Dudley   Roscrea
    Thos. Wilson   "   Thos. Darcey   Gorey

15-16

(a) Ship Marcus Hill, from Londonderry, arrived at New York on November 14, 1815.

(c)
John Lockhart
Margaret Lockhart
Robert Boyle
Thomas Stewart
Robert M'Intire
Robert Lowden
James Brooks
Gideon M'Miller
Robert Henderson
Patrick M'Gloughlin
Dennis M'Gloughlin
Mary M'Gloughlin
James Armstrong
Joseph Funston
John Funston
Anne Funston
Francis Funston
Margaret Maxwell
William Collins
William Smyth
John Crocket
James Crocket
James M'Intire
Stephen Todd
James Brown
James Armstrong
Thomas Nickle
Samuel M'Intire
Robert Funston
John Gallagher
William Bruce
William Galbraith
Charles Galbraith
James M'Gowan
William Gillilan
Daniel M'Shane
Richard Goodman
Catherine Goodman
Charles Cowan
William Britton
Isabella Bogle

* John Bogle
* Samuel Bogle
James Forsyth
Patrick Rodgers
Thomas M'Collison
David M'Collison
William Scott
* Jane Scott
Catherine Mechan
John Wilson
Robert Quinton
Hugh Cannon
William Crawford
Robert Kyle
Elizabeth Kyle
Patrick Flaherty
James Holmes
James Knox
Isabella Alexander
George Holmes
Robert M'Glaughlin
Catherine Scott
G. Gault
William Wright
William Collins
Mr. Irvine
James Ware
William Burns
Andrew Laird
Dary Irvine
James Wray
Catherine Kerr
Isabella Kerr
* Matilda Kerr
* James Kerr
* John Kerr
* Alexander Kerr
William Irvine
Samuel Buchanan
John Stoop

Michael Doak
Margaret Doak
William Wray
Robert Kernaghan
John Donaghy
Anne Donaghy
* Anne Donaghy
Isabella Gillespic
Samuel Love
Anne Love
Daniel Logan
David Patterson
Patrick Graham
Robert Carter
Mathew Ferguson
Samuel M'Fadden
Hugh Burns
John Frame
William Johnston
Hugh Fevry
Hugh Gallagher
Samuel Blair
Thomas Logan
Joseph Thompson
William M'Neremon
Christopher Henderson
John Henderson
Catherine Henderson
Anne Henderson
Jane Henderson
* Francis Henderson
Joseph Henderson
John Henderson
* George Henderson
* William Henderson
James Irvine
John Irvine
Hugh Scott
Daniel M'Colim
Margaret M'Colim

* children

15-17

(a) Brig Orient, from Dublin, arrived at New York on November 18, 1815.

(c)
Anne Kelly		James Frayne	Dublin
and child	Dublin	William Frayne	"
* John Field	"	Edward Codd	Wexford
William Henderson	Belfast	James Codd	"
Miles E. O'Reilly	Dublin	Michael Langley	
Christopher Nowlin	"	(teacher)	Dublin
Edward Pilkington		Wm. Withers	
(surgeon)	Dublin	(gun smith)	Belfast
George Byrne	"	John Brown	Cavan
John Dillon		Margaret Brown	
(sadler)	Dublin	and child	Cavan
John Waterson	Belfast	Michael Fagan	
* Thomas Salter	Dublin	(joiner)	Dublin
Patrick Hoye	"	Hugh Kelly	Carlow
William Tindall	"	Robert Johnston	
Michael Downey		(weaver)	Cavan
(millwright)	Dublin	Charles Conolan	Ballybay
* Mrs. Jane Maiben		James Conolan	"
and child	----	John Murray	Banbridge
* Richard Maiben	New York	William Templeton	Belfast
Charles Doyne		Anne Lambert	Birr
(taylor)	Dublin		

* American Citizens

15-18

(a) Ship Westpoint, from Belfast, arrived at New York on November 22, 1815.

(c)
John F. Walker	Rich Hill	Isabella O'Donnell	Randlestown
Samuel D. Moore	Carrickfergus	+ Mary O'Donnell	"
Alexander Dallas	Coleraine	Rose M'Keon	"
* William Chestnut	"	Fortescue Haslett	Belfast
* David Bell	Belfast	William Shanks	
William Mackeon	Ballymena	and wife	Dromore
Isabella Mackeon	"	James Carlisle	Ballynahinch
Alexander Stewart	Drumbridge	John Carlisle	"
James Barnett	Ballyagherty	Bernard Millgan	"
James R. Barnett	Belfast	William Sloan	Armagh
* Robert Sterling	Derry	William Clark	Stonyford
Mr. Armstrong		Francis Atkinson	Loughgall
and family	Ballynahinch	James M'Quoid	Clogher
James Ball	"	Patrick M'Kennon	Monaghan
James Moore	Donoughmore	Bernart M'Kennon	"
William Moore	"	Matthew Fitzgerald	Larne
Robert Moore	"	Alexander M'Dowell	Dromore
Margaret Moore	"	James Dripps	Maghera
James Beggs	Tullyleck	John M'Curdy	Ballycastle
Samuel M'Gladery	Stillwater	Neil M'Curdy	"
James Steel	Larne	Archibald Black	Rathlin
Thos. M'Vicker	"	John Rogers	Ballinahinch
Felix Gilmour	Randlestown	* American citizens	
Michael Gilmour	"	+ children	

(a) Ship Sally, 70 days from Dublin, arrived at New York on November 24, 1815.

(c)
Right Rev. Dr. Connoly	* Eliza Galbraith	Robert Farns
William Madigan	William Moore	Ellen Farns
Ally Madigan	John Moore	Mary Farns
Bridget Walsh	Peter Fox	Thomas Lynch
Walter Madigan	John Smyth	Patrick Lynch
Edward Madigan	Francis Gillin	John Clark
* James Madigan	Margaret Gillin	Michael O'Brien
* Mary Madigan	James Gillin	Margaret O'Brien
* Peggy Madigan	Margaret Kennedy	John O'Brien
* Judy Madigan	John Fitzgerald	John Moffat
* Anne Madigan	Mary Fitzgerald	William Moffat
Walter Madigan	John Gilmore	James Galbreath
Bridget M'Mahon	Andrew B. Burns	Rachel Galbreath
John Erwin	James Veatch	Patrick Brogan
* Mary Erwin	Patrick Danaho	James M'Grath
Mary Erwin	James Slavin	James Ryan
Eliza Walsh	Michael Slavin	Ellen Ryan
William Galbraith	Catherine Slavin	Joshua Brown
Anne Galbraith	* Anne Slavin	Andrew Brown

* children

(a) Ship Minerva, from Liverpool, arrived at New York before December 2, 1815.

(c)
John Given	Ireland	Thomas Bropigan	Ireland
John Deyr	"	James Handerson	"

(a) Barque Courier, from Lisbon, arrived at New York before December 2, 1815.

(c)
Mr. Lynch	Dublin	Mr. Casey	Dublin
Mr. Barrow	"	Mr. Allen	Ireland

(a) Brig Favorite, from Demerara, arrived at New York before December 2, 1815.

(c) Frindley Shields   Ireland

(a) Ship Emperor Alexander, from Londonderry, arrived at New York on November 25, 1815.

(c)

John Holmes	Raphoe	* Jane Brown	Belfast
George Ramsey	Coleraine	Richard Harcourt	Bushill
George Osborne	Dromore	Anne Harcourt	"
Robert M'Grier	Armagh	Rebecca Sinton	"
Robert Irvine	Ballindrate	Henry Sinton	"
John M'Lachling	Derry	John Sinton	"
James Douglass	"	Joseph Sinton	"
Samuel Keen	Augher	James Sinton	"
Thomas Wood	Auchnacloy	Anne Loony	"
Robert Gault	Coleraine	Susan Thornberry	"
Thompson Gault	"	John Lester	Strabane
Ezekiel Caldwell	Derry	Anne Lester	"
Alexander Cunningham	Aughnacloy	Alexander Moore	Derry
Archibald Sweeny	Burligh	Jane Moore	"
Anne Sweeny	"	George Kirkpatrick	Ringsend
Mary Sweeny	"	Thomas H. Chambers	Aughterm
Andrew Sweeny	"	Thomas Dowe	"
William Sweeny	"	Adam Christa	Ballymena
Thomas Wallace	Dromor	Thomas Murrin	Derry
Hannah Wallace	"	William Kirk	Buncrana
Robert Smyth	"	Roger Gallagher	Derry
Samuel Moore	Claugh	William Gallagher	Strabane
Letty Moore	"	Alexander Grier	Derry
James Owens	Armagh	James Dougherty	"
Nathaniel Carr	Ballybuny	Bridget Dougherty	"
William Anderson	Lettermuck	Bernard M'Gowen	Newtown Steward
Alexander Anderson	"	John Magill	Killetter
William Anderson	"	Patrick Murray	Auchinloe
Eliza Anderson	"	William Calhoun	Ballymena
Jane Anderson	"	James Calhoun	"
Seth Brown	Boston	Patrick Gallagher	Bellybeggs
Julia Brown	Belfast	James Houston	Strabane

(a) Ship Leda, Captain John Forsyth, from Newry, landed on Long Island on December 4, 1815.

(b) Went aground at 5 o'clock on the morning of December 4, on the south side of Long Island, opposite Southampton, carrying 60 passengers and a cargo of dry-goods. The passengers were landed safely.

(c) The following list of passengers was copied by the Shamrock from an advertisement published in the Long Island Star, exonerating Captain Forsyth from any blame in the grounding.

Owen Davis	John Thompson	John Graham
Bernard Phillips	James Clarke	Robert Hale
John Montgomery	David Medile	Thomas Morrow
Thomas Andrews	Robert Dycle	Patrick Murphy
Robert Andrews	Michael Wright	Henry Gray
Wm. Andrews sen.	Robert Jack	William Moore
Wm. Andrews jun.	Robert Gibson	John Dycle
Robt. Andrews		

(a) Brig Shannon, from Belfast, arrived at New York on January 18,11816.

(c)

Samuel Hopkins	Ballycastle	Bernard Magee	Dublin
Geo. Thompson	Antrim	Isaac Kield	"
Samuel Luke	Belfast	John Warnock	"
Ellen Farrell	Tyrone	Alexander Fair	"
Archibald Campbell	Antrim	Daniel Magill	"
James Carson	Belfast	Lewis Crawley	"
John Strean	Newtownards	Michael Crawley	"
Thomas Abbott	Kisburn	John Moore	"
Charles M'Ilroy	Down	Thomas M'Kell	New York
Mrs. M'Ilroy	"	John Gordon	Dumfries, Scotland
Alexander Ardis	Antrim	Elizabeth Gordon	"
Andrew Stavely	"	John Gordon	"
Catherine Nasida	Dublin	Michael Taylor	Perth, Scotland
Peter Stanley	"	Joseph Day Francis	Bath, England
Alexander M'Cracken	Belfast	Mrs. Day Francis	Liverpool
Joseph M'Cracken	"	Redmond Day Francis	"
Alexander M'Cracken jr.	"		

(a) Ship Ontario, from Dublin, arrived at New York on January 19, 1816.

(c)

Charles Purcel	Limerick	Patrick Rechil	Longford
Sarah Purcel	"	Michael M'Narney	"
James Andre	Dublin	Michael Mulligan	"
William Arnold	"	D. Spelman	"
Thomas Barbadge	"	T. M'Carfin	"
James Jones	"	Patrick Molloghan	"
Richard White	"	John O. Hanlon	"
Eliza Doyle		Peter Narey	Westmeath
and child	"	James Graham	"
James Bridges	"	Hugh Martin	Kildare
Anne Bridges	"	Marcella Martin	"
John Healy	"	Mary Byrne	
Margaret Callaghan		and 3 children	"
and two children	"	Fany Purcell	"
M. R. Walsh	Sligo	T. M'Daniel	"
James Arnold	Cavan	Mrs. M'Daniel	
John Brady	"	and child	"
Susan Brady	"	Catherine Calshan	Queen's Co.
Anne Brady	"	Geo. Steward	Monaghan
Alice Wheelock	Wexford	Tho. M'Daniel	Kilkenny
Patrick Doyle	"	And'w M'Daniel	"
Moses Doyle	"	James Madden	Slain
Paul Doran	"	Sam'l Benton	Mountrath
Robert Poole	"	Thomas Allen	King's Co.
Patrick Slattery	Tipperary	Daniel Asley	Manchester, England
John Stram	Fernagh	Peter Pitman	Nova Scotia
John M'Narney	Longford		

16-3

(a) Ship Amphion, from Dublin, arrived at New York on March 7, 1816.

(c)
George Andrews	Hugh Hughes	Mrs. Leddy
Thomas M'Lean	Sarah O'Neill	and 2 children
Nathl. M'Manns,	Edward Hobbart	Mathw. Clock
wife & 2 children	James Mackeson	and wife
Thos. Morrow	Wm. Evans	* Hugh Brady
Geo. Fenton	* Bernd. Fitzpatrick	
		* children

16-4

(a) Ship Erin, Captain John O'Connor, from Dublin, arrived at New York on March 11, 1816.

(c)
Richard Dillon	* Eliza Duigan	Jas. Murray
James Dillon	Wm. Rankin	Jas. West
Ellen Dillon	John Byrne	Geo. Rose
Catherine Cummins	Jas. Kelly	Edwd. Burke
Patk. Flanagan	Wm. Grady	Patk. Hogan
Patk. M'Dermott	Matthew Bohan	John Connor
Mary Kehoe	Philip Connor	Joseph Clegg
Patk. Byrne	Michl. Devlin	Jos. Atkinson
Wm. Duigan	Richd. Fegan	+ David Atkinson
* Anne Duigan	Michl. Connor	* children
* Bridget Duigan	John Marfelt	+ Citizen of the U.S.

16-5

(a) Ship Dublin Packet, from Dublin, arrived at New York on April 3, 1816.

(c)
Mrs. E. W. William	Dublin	Ellen Berney	Cavan
Simeon Rafferty	"	Michael Kenny	"
William O'Hara	"	Terence Fitzpatrick	"
Margaret Kennedy	"	William Ward	Carlow
Adam M'Cuthen	"	Michael Brophy	"
Pierce Asple	"	Thomas Binne	"
Richard Jordan	"	James Burn	"
John Mead	"	John W. Carle	Limerick
John Maly	"	Michael Carle	"
Thomas Whalen	"	Moses Carney	Wexford
James Fitzpatrick	"	Michael Carney	"
+ James M'Auley	Castleblaney	Philip Carney	"
Thomas Fitzgerald	Queen's Co.	John Carney	"
Sally Fitzpatrick	"	Patrick Carney	"
* Dennis Fitzpatrick	"	Eliza Carney	"
* Thomas Fitzpatrick	"	Mary Carney	"
* Mary Ann Fitzpatrick	"	Anne Carney	"
Daniel Phalen	"	Edmund Fitzpatrick	Kilkenny
Martin Loughman	"	# Michael Gorman	"
Thomas Berney	Cavan	* children; + U.S. citizen; # clergyman

85

16-6

(a) Ship Anne, from Cork, arrived at New York on April 13, 1816.

(c)
Y. Vaughan	Eliza Hendrick	Robert Boyd
James Vaughan	James Casey Barry	Frances Murphy
Thomas Vaughan	T. Ragan	Richard Willis
James Roche	William Long	Eleanor Willis
William Roche	John Kynn	James Wilis
Patrick Geary	Richard Duncan	Samuel Aidwell
Daniel Walsh	Jeremiah Sullivan	John Cole
John Byrne	Richard Dennison	Mary Sheehey
James Flyn	John Forest	* Samuel Bare
Coleman Riordan	Mich. Kerby	* Daniel Duneen
John Hendrick	F. Mahony	* Citizens of the l

16-7

(a) Brig Hannah, Captain Delano, 56 days from Dublin, arrived at New York on April 25, 1816.

(c)
Margaret Kelly	Mount Melick	Joseph Caldwell	Dublin
William Garelan	Co. Cavan	+ John O. Bream	"
John Brady	"	Thomas Ganly	Co. Antrim
Francis Coyle	Co. Fermanagh	Michael Tighe	"
William Wilson	Co. Antrim	John Ganly	"
John Banin	Co. Kilkenny	James Moody	Armagh
Pack Flurn	Dublin	Alfred Cheetham	Cheshire, England
James Read	"	John Taylor	" "

+ U.S. citizen.

16-8

(a) Ship Lorenzo, from Belfast, arrived at New York on May 2, 1816.

(c)
Abraham Bell	New York
Mary C. Bell	Stramore, Co. Down
* Rebecca H. Bell	"
* Thomas C. Bell	"
Jacob Harvey	Limerick
Catherine M'Mullen	Lurgan, Co. Armagh
Henry Quinn	"
Fras. Minnis	Saintfield, Co. Down
William Hay	Carrickfergus, Co. Antrim
John Moore	Belfast
Jess M'Murray	"
Saml. Bloomfield	"
Hugh Greene	"
John Farmer	"

John Kirkpatrick	Belfast
* Rob. Kirkpatrick	"
Margt. Kirkpatrick	"
* Mary Kirkpatrick	"
* Anne Kirkpatrick	"
* Jane Kirkpatrick	"
* Rebecca Keith	"
Robert M'Gill	Cookstown, Co. Derry
John Henry	"
Hugh Dawson	Carnmoney, Co. Antrim
James Graham	"
Sarah Dawson	"
+ David M'Murray	Ballybay, Co. Monaghan
Robert Ballagh	"
Fobert E. Ballagh	"
James Ballagh	"
James Erwin	"
James Markey	"
Margaret Miller	"
Ellen M'Geoch	"
Benjamin Miller	Cothill, Co. Monaghan
John Davison	Stramore, Co. Down
* Christ. Davison	"
James Fay	Castleblaney, Co. Monaghan
Cath. Ash	"
Neil Deavlin	Derry
Danl. Deavlin	"
Patrick Rogers	"
Hugh Rooney	Melanadony, Co. Leitrim
Daniel M'Alister	Donegal, Co. Antrim
Mat. Calney	Ballyshannan, Co. Donegal
Anthony Cassady	" °
Sam. M'Geoch	Newton Stuart, Wigtonshire
James Watson	Newtownards, Co. Down
George Workman	Tamletocrilly, Co. Derry
Sarah Davison	Gilford, Co. Down
Grace M'Geoch	Glymluse, Wigton Shire
John Donnelly	Stuartstown, Co. Tyrone
Hugh Peirie	Donaghy, Co. Tyrone

* Children
+ U.S. citizen

(a) Brig Nancy, from Newry, arrived at Philadelphia on May 4, 1816.

(c)
Margaret Watts	Tyrone	Bernard Halpin	Drogheda
Charles Watts	"	William Flinn	Banbridge
Joseph Watts	"	Rev. A. Wilson	Jonesborough
James Watts	"	William Martin	Market hill
Jane Watts	"	James Martin	"
Mary Watts	"	Chr. Boyle	Armagh
Daniel Acheson sen.	Letterkenny	Margaret Anderson	Derry
David Acheson jr.	"	Rachel Wigging	Monaghan
Mary Acheson	"	John Logan	"
Ellen M'Caskey	Aughnacloy	John M'Cauly	Lurgan
John M'Caskey	"	Jane M'Cauly	"

16-10

(a) Ship Globe, 45 days from Newry, arrived at Baltimore on May 4, 1816.

(c)
+ Rev. Robert Elliot, Chaplain to the U.S. Army		Hugh Porter, wife and 4 children	Dramore, Co. Down .
Richd. Mullan	Monaghan	John Parker	"
Patrick Kerr	"	Joseph Holmes	"
Canlan Rice	Ballybay,	Mary Canghey	"
Peter Black	Co. Monaghan	John O'Neil	Rostrevor, Co. Do
Pat. M'Cabe		Ellen M'Guire	Mullingar,
Samuel M'Cannell	Clare, Co.		Co. Westmeath
Carry M'Cannell	" Armagh	+ Alex. Graham and wife	
Adam Reid	" "		
John Sampson	Ballygalley, Co. Tyrone	+ Citizens of the U.S.	

88

(a) Brig Elizabeth, from Belfast, arrived at New York on May 5, 1816.

(c)

John Christy	Joseph Allen	James Abercromby
Robert Christy	Eliz. Allen	Robert Abercromby
Jane Christy	* George Allen	John Gibson
Elizabeth Christy	+ James Allen	Robert Newberry
* Adam Christy	* Mary Allen	Margaret Sleith
* Robert Christy	Alex. M'Call	* John Sleith
Catherine Minis	Alice M'Call	Joshua Willes
+ Robert James	William Orr	* Mary Willes
John James	Elizabeth Orr	Thomas Brankin
Joseph James	* Anne Orr	Bernd. Magee
William James	James Orr	William Harper
* John James	Jane Orr	Isaac Grey
+ Elizh. James	* George Orr	Mathan Wright
+ Mary James	Thomas Orr	James Peacock
Elizh. James	Robert Marrow	Thomas King
+ Jane James		

* Children + U.S. citizens.

(a) Ship Dido, from Newry, arrived at Philadelphia on May 6, 1816.

(c)

James Crooks	Moneymore Co. Derry	Patrick Rice	Camlagh, Co. Armagh
James Maxwell	Armagh	James Mullan	Roughforth, Templepatrick
James Armstrong	Port Norris	Patrick Hammill	Portadown
John Auchanan	"	Isabell Maxwell	Armagh
John Clark	Aughnamulin, near Ballybay	John Reed	----
John Henderson	----	John M'Kinstry	----
John Patterson	Port Norris	James Brown	Co. Down
Johnston Kearney	Armagh	Patrick Rea	----
Andrew Boyd	Camlagh, Co. Armagh	James Stuart	Hill-Hall, Co. Down
Hugh Finigan	----	Agnes Quin	Port Norris, Co. Down
Alexander Harper	Shea Bridge, Co. Down		
Joseph Morrow	Donaghmore, Co. Down		

16-13

(a) Brig John, from Belfast, arrived at New York on May 10, 1816.

(c)
Robert M'Canly	Co. Down	Rich. M'Canbrey	Co. Antrim
William Law	"	William Whitford	"
David Prey	"	James Sweeny	"
Adam Malcomson	"	William Beatty	Co. Fermanagh
Daniel M'Ginnis	Co. Antrim	Thomas Gallagher	Co. Sligo
Joseph M'Collum	"	William Murray	Co. Armagh
Thos. Martin	"	Marg. Murphy	
David Hewit	"	and 2 children	Co. Tyrone
John M. Roberts	"		

16-14

(a) Brig Charles Fawcett, from Dublin, arrived at New York on May 12, 1816.

(c)
Patrick Riall	Dublin	Patrick Fortune	Co. Wexford
John Byrne	"	Dennis Murphy	"
Robert Kelly	"	Mary Murphy	"
Bridget Murphy	"	Patrick Hayden	"
John Browne	"	James Sculler	"
* James Murphy	"	John Doyle	"
David Lain	"	Margaret Doyle	"
Anne Burke	"	James Kelly	"
Robert Smith	"	Martin Murphy	"
Martin Doyle	Strabane	James Bradley	Liverpool
Peter M'Kevers	Co. Louth	James Hanff	Co. Westmeath
+ ---- Farrell	Philadelphia	+ Peter Duffy	Dundalk
+ ---- Perrin	"	+ Morris Murphy	New York
* + Fanny Prain	"	Catherine Murphy	Carlow
Patrick Magee	Kilkenny	Peter Lynes	New York
John Magee	"	* children; + U.S. citizens	

16-15

(a) Brig Hare, from Galway, arrived at New York on May 12, 1816.

(c)
Thomas Dew	Thomas Cummins	* Patrick Nalty
John Craven	Martin Higgins	* Margaret Nalty
Garrit Fahey	James Laffey	* Mary Nalty
Patrick Connell	John Concannon	Michael Cay
Patrick Coghlan	Willm. Concannon	P. Nolan
Catherine Coghlan	James Daniel	* Eliza Coghlan
Bridget Coghlan	Mary Fahey	* Mary Coghlan
* Catherine Coghlan	James Cay	Lawrence O'Brien
John M'Cormik	Thomas Nalty	Mary O'Brien
Tim. T. Fahey	Bridget Nalty	

90

(a) Ship Active, from Londonderry, arrived at Philadelphia on May 13, 1816.

(c)
James Gowan	Joseph Anderson	William Anderson,
William M'Grath	Patrick M'Arand	mother and brother
George Record	Anne Duffin	Eleanor Crumley
William Dougherty	Mary Heely	and sister
Eleanor M'Key	Robert M'Cauly	William Sharkey
Laetitia Quinn	and brother	and sister
James Davenport	Anne Crawford	
John Dixon	and 3 children	

16-17

(a) Ship Louisa, from Dublin, arrived at Philadelphia on May 17, 1816.

(c)
John Flynn	Balbrigan	Joseph Mahon	Kilkenny
Mary Flynn	"	Maurice Hicks	"
John Flynn jr.	"	Patrick Nevin	"
Patrick Dillon	"	Peter Monaghan	King's Co.
James Lyndon	Dublin	John Walsh	Tipperary
Michael Neal	"	James Tennaly	Co. Meath
Margaret Flaherty	"	Robert Sherlock	"
James Finn	"	William Murray	Carlow
Wilson A. Hunt	"	Daniel Murray	"
Adam Lett	"	Nathaniel Budden	Cavan
Nicholas O'Neal	"	Mary Lyndon	----
Patrick Brown	Kilkenny	Anne O'Neal	----
Catherine Mahon	"	Thomas Reilly	----

16-18

(a) Ship Aeolus, from Newry, arrived at New York before June 1, 1816.

(c)
Robert McKee	Mary Davis	Anne Johnston
Edward Byrne	Thomas Harrison	Margaret Bolton
James Harrison	J. Kidd	John George
Robert Jolly	Bernard McCann	B. Toner
Margaret Jolly	Owen McCann	John Murphy
Catharine Robertson	Henry Wright	Patrick Crawlon
Hugh Byrnes	Owen McArdle	Patrick McQuinn
Mary Byrnes	Anne McArdle	Michel Garney
Patrick Flanagan	Mary Anne McArdle	John McColley
Samuel Hill	John McArdle	James McLaughlin
J. Arnold	Peter McArdle	William Seeds
Thomas Bacon	Thomas Catherwood	Owen McEvoy

16-19

(a) Brig London, from Newry, arrived at New York on June 1, 1816.

(c) | | | | |
|---|---|---|---|
| + John J. Jacques | Monmouth, N.J. | Bernard M'Manus | Cavan |
| + William Trotter | " | William Lyons | Armagh |
| David Ferris | Newry | A. Adair | Kilkeel, Co. Dow |
| Robert Kelly | Banbridge | William M'Kee | " |
| James Borr | Portadown, Co. | Robert Hanna | " |
| Henry Sanderson | "   Armagh | John Amact | " |
| William Gilmore | " | Thomas Austin | " |
| Margaret Gilmore | " | Rebecca Austin | " |
| William Gilmore jr. | " | William Gordon | " |
| Patrick Murney | Dublin | Francis Morton | " |
| Patrick Rafferty | Drogheda | Arthur Thompson | Liverpool |
| Matthew Finigan | " | hon Hill | " |

+ U.S. citizens

16-20

(a) Brig Wilson, from Dublin, arrived at New York on June 1, 1816.

(c) | | | | |
|---|---|---|---|
| William M'Kay | Co. Dublin | John Pierce | Co. Wexford |
| James M'Kay | " | Martin Murphy | " |
| Eliza M'Kay | " | James Clancey | " |
| Ellen Hawthorn | " | Susan Murphy | " |
| James Wade & wife | Dublin | Catherine Dixon | " |
| John Winstanley | " | David Roche | " |
| Thomas Duff | " | John Roche | " |
| John Duff | " | Daniel Langton | Kilkenny |
| Jane Duff | " | Thomas Bambrick | " |
| Margaret Duff | " | Michael Byrne | Carlaw |
| Thomas Hatch | " | Margaret Rowan | Mountrath |
| + Owen M'Dermott | New York | John Rowan | " |
| Jeremiah Wardle | Lancashire | Mary Morris | Wexford |
| Thomas Kehoe | Co. Wexford | Richard Sinnot | " |
| + Francis Rochford | " | James Corish | " |
| William Harpur | " | John Furlong | " |
| William Kinshela | " | Joseph Connor | " |
| William Pether | " | James Cosgrave | " |
| James Walsh | " | + U.S. citizens | |

16-21

(a) Ship **Conistoga**, Captain Burk, from Dublin, arrived at Philadelphia on June 2, 1816.

(b) The date given in the Shamrock is clearly June 2, but the list was published in the edition of June 29, which could indicate that the "2" was an error for some date between "20" and "29".

(c)
Arthur Doly	Margaret West	Florena Ingram
Henrietta Doly	the younger	Mary Ingram
Henrietta Doly	Wm. West	Sally Ingram
the younger	John West	Florena Ingram
Jane Doly	Elizabeth Rielly	Mary Ingram
Altha Doly	Rose Rielly	Farmer Ingram
Maria Doly	Eliza Rielly	John Ingram
John Stasey	Jeremiah Brophy	Francis Humphreys
Sarah Stasey	Thomas Jordain	Robert Guirson
Eliza Stasey	Peter Allen	Caroline Weeks
Wm. Stasey	Hannah Allen	Jane Weeks
Doritha Stasey	Peter H. Allen	Frances Weeks
Margaret Stasey	Henry S. Allen	Thos. Weeks
George Warrier	Mathew Hopkins	Philip Bradley
James Flinn	Peter M'Demiott	Val. Kennady
Margaret West	Josiah Borlridge	

16-22

(a) Ship Foster, from Londonderry, arrived at New York on June 4, 1816.

(c)
Thomas Hawkins	Washington Baird	* Susannah M'Dermott
Michael Canigan	Samuel Cochran	Rose M'Dermott
Charles M'Coal	Robert M'Farland	William M'Dermott
William Curry	Alexander M'Cay	James Blair
* Alexander Curry	Patrick Burns	James Elder
Patrick M'Coal	Matthew Glassey	John M'Menamy
Margaret Fisher	Robert Glassey	Peter M'Menamy
* Michael Fisher	Kearns Fulton	James M'Redden
* Hugh Fisher	Catherine Fulton	John M'Daid
Peter M'Laughlin	Joseph Given	James Wallace
Francis Campbell	Patrick Diver	David Quigley
Catherine Calgan	Elizabeth Carr	Alexander Miller
Mary Calgan	Anne Dogherty	Bryan Doherty
John O'Hare	Patrick M'Dermott	Catherine Reynolds
James Clements	Mary M'Dermott	James Gamble
Margaret Clements	* Charles M'Dermott	* - Fulton, three
Alexander Limerick	* William M'Dermott	months old
	* Children	

(a) Ship Westpoint, from Belfast, arrived at New York on June 5, 1816.

(c)

Simpson Shepherd	Co. Derry	Margaret Kelly	Co. Down
Jane Shepherd	Co. Tyrone	Thomas Spratt	"
* Richard Shepherd	Co. Armagh	Mary Spratt	"
* Margaret Shepherd	"	Hugh Clark	"
Catherine Sloan	Co. Antrim	Hugh Carslile	"
* Catherine Sloan	"	Joseph Weathers	"
Alexander Service	"	Moses Parker	"
Felix M'Cam	"	Henry Creen	"
Alexander Mooney	"	William Gracey	"
Mary Mooney	"	Arthur M'Tea	"
Thomas Boyd	"	John Turley	"
William Manning	"	* Sarah Turley	"
Martha M'Clushey	"	Eliza Turley	"
* Matilda M'Clushey	"	Anne Turley	"
Johh Fearis	Co. Down	Sarah Turley	"
Margaret Fearis	"	George Herran	"
Catherine Fearis	"	Arthur Charters	"
Margaret Fearis	"	William M'Bride	Co. Armagh
John Fearis	"	John Stilt	"
Mary Fearis	"	James Wilson	"
John M'Dowell	"	Sarah Wilson	"
John Murdoch	"	* Children.	
Jane Smyth	"		

(a) Ship Enterprise, from Londonderry, arrived at New York on June 10, 1816.

(c)

William Coach	John Robinson	James Cunningham
Isabella Coach	John M'Gavaran	Thomas Cunnay
John Coach	John Scott	John Scott
Gera Johnston	Edwd. Morgan	Chs. M'Braty
Mary Johnston	Neal O'Boyle	Thomas Quince
D. Robertson	Moses Cannon	Patk. Faulkender
Eleanr. Robertson	Mathew Tigut	Patk. O'Donnell
William Johnston	Daniel M'Gattiger	John Burr
Oliver Johnston	James Martin	John Mulholland
Samuel Spencer	James Conolly	John Carney
Moses Black	John Russell	Patk. Carrigan

16-25

(a) Brig **Falcon**, from Londonderry, arrived at New York before June 15, 1816.

(b) The O'Shaughnessy's names are marked "Limerick". A note is added: "Mrs. O'Shaughnessy was delivered of a fine boy on George's Bank on the evening of the 6th inst...."

(c)		
Marcus Wilson	Andrew Moore	Martin Graham
Michael Gallagher	James Huey	David Park
John Gilfillin	Betty Huey	Cornelius M'Laughlin
John Wiley	David Park	John Toland
Henry Griffiths	Henry Kerr	John McCann
William Shields, Senr.	Nancy Kerr	Samuel Baird
William Shields, Jur.	Thomas Kerr	William Whiteside
Alexander Boggs	John Kerr	Hugh Gallagher
James Green	Robert Kerr	Betsey Gallagher
James Alexander	Mary Malsey	Michael O'Shaughnessy
Anne Alexander	John Hughes	Margaret O'Shaughnessy
Sarah Jane Alexander		

16-26

(a) Ship Jane, from Londonderry, arrived at Philadelphia on June 14, 1816.

(c)			
James Rowan	Belfast	Elizabeth Keys	Donegall
Ann Gray	Strabane	Robert Elliston	"
Hugh Fee	Donegall	Ann Gibson	Tyrone
Patrick M'Bride	"	James Crawford	Donegall
John Dougherty	"	Mary Crawford	"
William Hamilton	"	James Fergue	"
Ann Brown	Tyrone	Eliza Fergue	"
Wister Galey	"	George Kirkpatrick	N.S. Stewart
William Galey	"	John M'Colgan	Donegall
John M'Farlane	Magherafelt	Michael Carey	"
Henry Harbison	"	Edward Diver	"
Alexander Russell	Donegall	Hugh Tierney	"
Francis Russell	"	James Campbell	Philadelphia
James Russell	"	James Martin	N.S.Stewart
Jane Russell	"	Elizabeth M'Cauley	"
John Russell	"	Eliza. M'Cauley	"
Samuel Keys	"		

16-27

(a) Schooner William, from Belfast, arrived at New York on June 15, 1816.

(c) Bernard Murray
Thomas Read
Samuel Dale
* William Dale
Daniel Dale
John Dale
John Conerry

William Clark
Daniel M'Dermott
William Burchill
Charles Rogan
John M'Gunnis
Thomas Wiley
Elizabeth Wiley

Ann Wiley
* Mary Wiley
* Jane Somerville
Mary Somerville
George Henderson
Thomas Henderson

16-28

(a) Ship Marcus Hill, from Londonderry, arrived at New York on June 15, 1816.

(c) Joseph Walker
Constantine Walker
George Walker
James Walker
Eliza Walker
* Mary Walker
* William Walker
Samuel Hill
Anne Hill
* Matilda Hill
Patrick Currant
Bridget Mullan
David Stewart
Catherine Harvey
Anne Harvey
Isabella Laughery
John Smith
Eliza Smith
Unity Brennan
John Stephens
Patrick M'Gowan
Dennis M'Gowan
William Stewart
Thoms. M'Granahan
Dennis M'Claskey
Henry M'Ginnis
Ellen M'Ginnis
Owen M'Ginnis
Thomas M'Hale
Mathew Brown
Patrick Cain
Edward M'Gloin
John Harkin
Charles Cain
Hugh Connor

John Calhoun
John Connor
Henry M'Claskey
John Lynch
Richard Connor
Susan Lynch
Robert Donnelly
James Donnelly
Patrick Donnelly
Arthur Quinn
John Doherty
Dominick M'Voy
Edward Scott
Andrew Corrigan
Daniel Doherty
Anne Doherty
Michael Doherty
Thomas Lecky
Charles Finlay
Patrick Duffy
Dennis M'Laughlin
Michael Dogherty
Patrick Coneghan
John Barr
William Bradley
Andrew Butler
Mary Butler
* Eliza Butler
Mathew Park
Edward Dally
Patrick Hulton
James Deary
David Doherty
Henry M'Gongle
John Rogers

William Bednard
William Doherty
Dudley Kelly
Patrick Kelly
Hugh Doherty
George M'Colgan
John M'Laughlin
James Revenaugh
Susan Diver
Sidney Diver
William Diver
* George Diver
* Mary Diver
George Borskin
David Crawford
James Mechan
John Elder
William Burk
Alexander Kennedy
James Carlin
James Donnell
William Brown
Hugh M'Menomy
Charles M'Fadden
Jane Kirkpatrick
Crissey Kirkpatrick
* Alex. Kirkpatrick
Eliza Kirkpatrick
* And. Kirkpatrick
Sarah M'Loughlin
John Carney
Robert Griswell
Mary Griswell
* William Griswell
John Griswell

Girzy Cafferty
Mary Cafferty
Philip Doherty
Thomas M'Ginnis
Thomas Banks
George Butler
Edward Hagan
John M'Bride
Daniel M'Ginnis
John Bayley
William Nickle
Henry Donaghe
Patrick Duffy
Fanny Duffy
Anne Derlin
Alexander Cathcart
Catherine Cathcart

John Shannan
Patrick Murphy
John Guthrey
William Thompson
Edward Lawn
Robert Story
William Anderson
Edward Callaghan
Hugh Hammond
Samuel Burnside
George Baird
William Garven
Mathew Shearer
Philip M'Laughlin
Dennis Coll
Joseph Gilmour
Alexander Love

Sarah Rankin
Samuel Brown
Anne Brown
* John Brown
* William Brown
* Mary Brown
George Laughlin
John M'Comb
Richmond Wantya
James Peden
James Ridge
Michael Laperty
Daniel M'Aloo
John Strawbridge
Jane White

* Children.

16-29

(a) Ship Niagra, from Londonderry, arrived at New York on June 17, 1816.

(c) John M'Crea
John M'Crea
Samuel Boyle
Patrick Fay
Daniel Donnell
George Carson
James Coulta
Peter Gallager
Bridget Gallager
Robert Simpson
John Crawford
Thomas Todd

James Hutton
Samuel Stewart
Robert Hay
William Thompson
Hugh Hammond
Samuel Gray
William Miller
John Thompson
William Hall
John M'Ilhames
James Pomeroy

John Millar
Robert Millar
---- Simpson
John Armstrong
George Gault
James Corry
Hugh M'Claskey
Henry Davis
Bernard Brown
Peter Bradley
Samuel Craig

(a) Brig Ossian, from Belfast, arrived at New York on June 20, 1816.

(c)

James Singer	Robert Reid	J. Crawford
Henry I. Granthorn	Rachel Reid	M. Crawford
Thos. H. O'Cain	* George Reid	Duncan Campbell
Henry O'Loone	James Henderson	M. M'Clean
Jamrs Creighton	William Henderson	S. Hughes
John Bailie	Eleanor Henderson	J. Hughes
William Bailie	Charles Chambers	W. Hamilton
* Robert Bailie	Eliza Chambers	James Reid
* Isabella Bailie	Archibald Caruthers	M. Reid
* James Bailie	M. Caruthers	Wm. Woodside
David Bailie	* Jane Caruthers	S. M'Kay
John Bailie	* John Caruthers	R. Woodside
Mary Anne Bailie	M. Shannon	Peter M'Keene
William J. Connolly	J. Diamere	R. Walker
B. Jameson	P. M'Kay	W. Cloane
John Mahany	W. Pole	J. Moone
Mary Mahany	W. M'Dowel	P. Boyd
* Mary J. Mahany	M. M'Dowel	H. Gibbons
* Mary Mahany	* John M'Dowel	J. Gibbons
Henry Mulholland	* C. M'Dowel	* M. Gibbons
Thomas Blair	C. M'Dowel	R. Warwick
John Buher	H. Bell	John Putledge
James Gillespie	John Noone	J. O'Neil
Eliza Gillespie	J. Carlton	C. Chesnut
*.Mary Anne Gillespie	M. Carlton	M. Chesnut
Mary Gillespie	J. Carlton	* S. Chesnut
Thomas Tiney	H. Walker	J. Morrison
Charles Hunter	M. Walker	R. Morrison
Catherine Hunter	J. Walker	James Jugant
Thomas Peid	* J. Walker	* James M'Clean

* Children

16-31

(a) Ship George, from Belfast, arrived at Philadelphia on June 24, 1816.

(c)
Robert Stewart	John Shaw	Jno. McCormick
Martha Stewart	Rose Shaw	Samuel Armstrong
Wm. Stewart	Wm. Shaw	Wm. Laughlin
Jane Stewart	Ann Shaw	John Hair
Alexander Stewart	Mary Shaw	Jas. Mitchell
Jno. Kearney	Rose Shaw	Alexander Kennedy
Henry Kearney	Robert Shaw	Wm. Doffin
Robert Hay	James Shaw	Wm. Adair
Alexander O'Neall	Thomas Shaw	James M'Cawley
Wm. M'Collough	Jas. M'Vea	Jno. Gausley
Alexander Swan	Jno. Meloy	Robert Dawson
David Swan	Robert Byers	E. Alexander
Margaret Swan	Robert Glass	Wm. Hamilton
John Swan	Esther Palmer	Eliza Hamilton
Margaret Swan	Margaret Palmer	James Nielson
Jas. Laughran		

16-32

(a) Brig Sophia, from Belfast, arrived at New York on June 26, 1816.

(c)
John Adams	John O'Neil, wife	John Carr
John M'Kinne	and child	Thos. Hill
S. Wallace	John Campbell	Adam Hill
W. Boyd	David Byers	Hugh Castlewood
J. Jameson	Thomas Wilson	James M'Culloch
and brother	James Bryd	James Fisher, wife
J. M'Garagher, wife	William Pettigrew	and five children
and five children	John Hetherington	James M'Cormick
John Phoenix	Joseph Burnside	Arthur Quin
James Anderson	and wife	John Devlin
M. O'Donnel	Peter Hughes	John Dickson
and wife	John M'Gra	Mary Rowan
John Hill	---- M'Keighan	and four children
John Tanner	Jas. M'Cambridge	Andrew M'Causland
Samuel Dickey	Matthew Campbell	Alexander Sparks,
Sarah Hetherington	---- Magher	Scotland
and five children	Rich. M'Allignon	John M'Dill, "
John Gitty	---- Bankhead	John Law, "
James Gitty	Stewart Rafferty	W. Millikin, "
James Gardner	John Martin	Eliza Sparks, "
Owen O'Neil, wife	Thomas Thompson	Eliza Beverly, "
and child		

99

(a) Brig Foundling, from Sligo, arrived at New York on June 30, 1816.

(c)			
Owen Canway	Mount Temple	Hugh Nesbit	Sligo
Catherine Canway	"	John Cannelan	"
* Mary Canway	"	Matthew Barbonr	Carney
Hugh Kilmartin	"	Thomas Little	"
Owen Freal	"	Patrick Kilmartin	Mullaghmore
Honor Freal	"	Hugh Kilmartin	"
Paul Gereghy	"	Mary Kilmartin	"
John Kilmartin	"	Hannah M'Kninon	"
John Burns	"	Dominick Flanagan	"
James Finlan	"	Thomas Bailie	Ballymote
Mary Finlan	"	Thomas Conolly	Darby
Patrick Finlan	"	Patrick M'Sherry	"
Owen Finlan	"	Eleanor Ferguson	Drumcliff
John Finlan	"	Edward Ferguson	"
Mary Finlan	"	John Ferguson	"
Bryan M'Garahy	"	Jeremiah Sweeny	Coolerrah
Bridget Finlan	"	Thomas Conolly	Carrick on Shanne
William Foley	"	Charles Kelly	"
Patrick Harkin	"	John M'Gowan	Dunally
John Kennedy	Grange	Patrick Gallagher	Teeling, Co. Done
Dominick Curred	"	James Cryan	Aughnasare, Co.
Bryan Curred	"	Mary Cryan	" Roscommor
Anne Kennedy	"	Michael Cryan	"
Bartholomew Curred	"	* Catherine Cryan	"
Michael Healy	"	* Mary Cryan	"
Bartholomew Clinton	"	* Patrick Cryan	"
Patrick Hargaden	"	Timothy Cryan	"
John Healy	"	Bridget Cryan	"
Mary Healy	"	Martin Cryan	"
Patrick Healy	"	Joseph Deighan	Dublin
Wm. M'Nulty	Tauly	Martin Gormley	Boyle
John Roony	"	James O'Neil	Ballymote
Sarah Roony	"	Luke Gore	
Margaret M'Gloin	"	John Campbell	
Thomas Castello	Magheraw	Peter Goveran	
Bryan Healy	"	Patrick Wynne	
Michael Castello	"	Michael Rooney	
Michael Feeny	"	John Hart	
Patrick Gillen	"	William Mechlan	
Michael Kelly	Drumahare	Mary Mechlan	
John Kelly	"	George Hill	Scotland
James M'Laughlin	"	Walter Scott	"
Joseph Flynn	"	John Mein	"
Charles Doherty	Coothall, Co.	Alexander Smith	"
	Roscommon	Andrew Beattie	"
Martin Golrich	Sligo		

6-34

(a) Brig Orient, from Sligo, arrived at New York on July 1, 1816.

(c)

Richard Taylor	Sligo	Patrick Carroll
Anne Galey	"	Mary Carroll
Eliza Galey	"	Terence Carroll
Esabella Lindsay	"	Francis Johnston
Jane Johnston	"	John M'Glam
Thomas Baland	"	Patrick M'Glam
Anne Foley	"	Roger Waters
Patrick Brennan	"	Catherine Bride
Mark Hart	"	John M'Gloin
William Johnston	"	John Waters
Elizabeth Johnston	"	Matthew Leary
* Johnston	"	Charles Mitchell
Hugh Flynn	Ballifarnan	James Henegan
John Higgins	"	John Lingan
Thomas Miller	Drimkeeran	Bridget Lingan
Thomas Young	"	Patrick Reynolds
Richard Edwards	Drimshambo	Michael Rooney
Edward Standford		William West
John Clancey		Anne West
John Christian		Alexander Young
Thomas Cook		Eliza Young and child
Margaret Hart		Robert Young
Bridget Hart		Patrick M'Gowan
William Conolly		Mary M'Guire
John Conolly		* Bridget M'Guire
M. Conolly		James Connellin
Mary M'Gloin and child		Bryan Queenan
* Henry M'Gloin		* Children.

16-35

(a) Ship Bristol, from Dublin, arrived at New York on July 1, 1816.

(c)

Richard Bernard	Charles Mahon	John Mulvey
James Nowland	Michael Leddy	* Isabella Mulvey
Patrick Kane	Berrard Petit	Edward Patterson
James Keirnan	Samuel Buttle	Peter Farrell
Thomas Brady	Margaret Buttle	Owen Farley
Michael Berry	Michael Corkoran	Francis Heany
Charles Wilson	John Harding	Thomas Martin
Robert Martin	William Flemming	John Dooney
John Hawthorn	Catherine Smith	Francis Berry
Bill Hawthorn	---- Smith	Joseph Reynolds
* Thomas Hawthorn	---- Smith	Eliza Reynolds
* Esther Hawthorn	James Brenan	Patrick M'Manus
* Patrick Smyth	Charles Masterson	Samuel Evins
* Terence M'Cabe	Patrick Masterson	Daniel Fitzpatrick
Patrick Gunn	Michael Mooney	Laurence Reynolds
Samuel Mite	John Mooney	* Children.

101

16-36

(a) Brig Ceres, from Dublin, arrived at Philadelphia on July 2, 1816.

(c)
Patrick Mulvaney	Dublin	Mathew Furlong	Wexford
William Stevens	Wexford	Edward Holden	"
Walter Rochford	"	Dennis Jordan	"
James Devereaux	"	Francis Tierney	Carlaw
M. Casher	"	Joseph Tierney	"
Bartholomew Casher	"	Margaret Tierney	"
Anne Casher	"	Thomas Kelly	"
Margaret Casher	"	Patrick Mullen	"
Martin Murphy	"	Edward Mullen	"
Bridget Murphy	"	Thomas Mullen	"
Mary Murphy	"	William Dunn	King's Co.
Simon Murphy	"	Elizabeth Dunn	"
Francis Murphy	"	Mathew Dunn	"
Johanna Murphy	"	Peter Dunn	"
John Murphy	"	Mary Dunn	"
Laurence Murphy	"	James Halpen	Kilkenny
Patrick Pettit	"	Nicholas Thornton	Dundalk
Andrew Cleary	"	John Thornton	"
Catherine Johnson	"		

16-37

(a) Ship Dibby and Eliza, from Dublin, arrived at New York on July 3, 1816.

(c)
George Thompson	Dublin	James Murphy	Carlow
Bartholomew Ellis	"	Cicily Murphy	"
Joseph Ellis	"	* Eleanor Murphy	"
John Burke	"	George Flushing	"
John Butterley	"	Eleanor Flushing	"
Mary Butterley	"	* John Flushing	"
James Finigan	"	Joseph Kennedy	"
Francis White	"	Margaret O'Reilly	"
Charles Hughes	"	* Eliza O'Reilly	"
Mrs. Aunis	"	* Hugh O'Reilly	"
Mrs. Ogilby	"	Edward O'Reilly	"
* John Ogilby	"	Anne Ivers	"
* Robert Ogilby	"	William Ivers	"
* Frederick Ogilby	"	* William Ivers	"
Eleanor Lucas	"	Anne Ivers	"
William Kelly	Carlow	* R. Ivers	"
Margaret Kelly	"	* Catherine Ivers	"
* Edward Kelly	"	John O'Neal	"
* John Kelly	"	John Ivers	"
* Adam Kelly	"	Samuel G. Ivers	"
John Kelly	"	William Ivers	"
Richard Kelly	"	* John Gibson	"
Margaret Kelly	"	George Twainley	Wicklow

16-37 (c), continued

Mary Twainley	Wicklow	Mary Hanley	Tipperary
* Jane Twainley	"	James Conry	Waterford
Thomas Bennett	Wexford	Eleanor Gonry	"
Thomas Halle	"	John Bradley	Navan
William Thomas	"	Nicholas Delany	Kilkenny
Charles Reilly	Meath	Thomas Beerman	Queen's Co.
Thomas Reilly	"	+ Samuel Warr	England
Matthew Kinanak	"	+ Eliza Warr	"
Langn. Kananak	Longford	+ * George Warr	"
James Hanley	Tipperary		

* Children. + U.S. Citizens.

16-38

(a) British Packet Montague, arrived at New York before July 6, 1816, via Halifax.

(c) James Callaghan   City of Kilkenny
    Patrick Fennely   "

16-39

(a) Brig Only Son, from Dublin, arrived at Philadelphia on July 6, 1816.

John Murray, wife and 2 children	Balbriggan	Owen Roundtree & wife, Dublin	
		George Ennis	Enniscorty
Christopher Cam, wife and son	"	James Hagan	"
		Miles Vaharty	"
James Callaghan	"	Thomas Muldary	Mullingar
Thomas Waldron	"	Danl. Lalor	Queen's Co.
Patrick Larkin	"	Hannah Latham	"
Thomas O'Connor	Dublin	Hugh Keating	King's Co.
Henry Leahy	"	John M'Lain	Drogheda
Edw. Brown	"	Bryan M'Grim	"
John O'Brien, wife and child	"	William Moore	Co. Cavan
		Thomas Campbell	Co. Tyrone

16-40

(a) Brig George, from Belfast, arrived at New York on July 8, 1816.

(c)
David Walker
Martha Walker
* Jane Walker
James Sloan
James Simpson
Hugh M'Laughlin
Margaret M'Laughlin
James Ross
Jane Mackerill
Thomas Mackerill
John Scilly
Jane Scilly
* Margaret Scilly
David Walker
Matthew M'Queen
Thomas M'Donnell
Robert M'Donnell
David Christy
Hugh M'Mail
John Davidson
Samuel Todd
James Murray
English Crawford
John Fife
Patrick M'Carker
William Chapman
Mary Fife
Eleanor Sweeny
Catharine Sweeny
Sarah Scott

Eliza Scott
Jane Scott
Robert Wilson
James M'Grery
Margaret M'Grery
Archibald M'Murry
William M'Lorran
George M'Conley
Anthony Doherty
Patrick Hughes
James Mackerill
Robert Temen
Hugh Rogers
Samuel Cairns
Mary Cairns
William Gorman
John Kingsland
Matthew Gilmore
John Gilmore
Hugh Gibson
Eliza Woods
Hugh Mollan
Daniel Stewart
Adam Atcheson
William Parr
Margaret Parr
Mary Parr
Thomas Parr
* Eliza Parr
* John Parr

* Anne Parr
* William Parr jr.
Robert Martin
George Martin
William Martin
James Gibson
Margaret Gibson
Robert Carr
Andrew M'Gowan
Alexander Watson
Matthew Clark
Margaret Clark
Jane Clark
M. Slinler
John Gilmore
Christopher Gilmore
Mary Gilmore
Thos. M'Kill
James Woods
Henry Wiggins
James Morer
Samuel Given
Matthew Morrison
John Cornwell
Andrew M'Affer
Agnes Allen
Thomas Hays
James M'Canaghty
Samuel Allen
David Campbell

* Children

16-41

(a) Brig Actress, from Dublin, arrived at New London on July 10, 1816.

(c)
John Lawler, wife
   and child   Co. Kildare
William Reynolds   "
Simon Donoher   "
Thos. Kervan, Phillipstown, Kings Co.
John Dempsey, Portarlington,   "
William O'Hara, Tallamore,   "
Michael Kelly   Co. Carlow
Patrick Newlan   "
Michael Kehoe   "
James Elms   "
Robert Duney   "
Mark Picket   "
John Warren   "

Edward Warren   Co. Carlow
Thomas Cook   "
Christopher Geohegan, Co. Dublin
Robert Wacum, wife
   and child   "
Charles Nowlan   "
---- Watesr   city of Dublin
---- M'Donnel   Co. Meath
---- Henry & dtr.   "
Terrence Sweeney
---- Hugh
Owen M'Dermott
John M'Dermott
Thomas Mason & wife

104

(a) British ship Prince of Brazil, from Belfast, arrived at New York on July 15, 1816.

(c)

William Marshall	Eliza Beatty	William Taggart
Hugh Aeggs	Susan Lindsay	and wife
Robert Tone	Margaret Wallace	Andrew M'Tice
Henry M'Tahan	James Gibson	Samuel Bell
and wife	John Kennedy	Wm. Bell
Hugh Dickson	and wife	John Walsh
Arthur Cotter	* William Kennedy	James Smith
* Jane Dickson	Thomas Crosby	John Stewart
* Eliza Dickson	Thomas Bell	and wife
* Mary Ann Dickson	Thomas Cosgrove	* Jane Stewart
* Sally Dickson	William Magee	John Magee
William Ferguson	James Magee	Wm. Ritchie
and wife	Wm. Simpson	John Ritchie
Esther Ferguson	and wife	Patrick Orr
* Sally Ferguson	Bernard M'Bride	Thomas Barker
* Eliza Ferguson	Peter Poland	Patrick M'Ilroy
* Mary Ann Ferguson	John Magee	John Diamond
* Susannah Ferguson	Robt. M'Intire	Samuel M'Gibbon
Samuel Dickson	John Martin	Patrick M'Cartney
Charles Gurroll	Alexr. Pierce	Martin Reed
Elijah Currell	Charles Money	John Fogers
* Susannah Currell	Margaret Money	and wife
A. M'Guskin	John Bradley	* Ann Rogers
James Maurice	Wm. Bradley	* Mary Rogers
John M'Cauly	Richard Drain	* Alexr. Rogers
Peter Curran	Matthew Wilson	James Bradford
Henry Connolly	James Ruddock	Allan Stewart
and wife	James Thompson	John Stewart
David Boyd	James Ferris	George Campbell
Samuel Boyd	John Young	Willism Riddle
Andrew Kennedy	John M'Daniel	Samuel Riddle
Jas. Beatty	William M'Quig	Joseph Johnson
David Beatty	John Drain	* Children.

(a) Ship Samuel, from Newry, arrived at New York before July 20, 1816.

(c) No list published.

(a) Ship Neptune, from Newry, arrived at New York before July 20, 1816.

(c) No list published.

(a) Ship Alpha, from Belfast, arrived at Philadelphia on July 22, 1816.

(c)

James Linchey	Philadelphia	John Johnson	Belfast
Thomas W. Scott	"	Daniel Blair	Carrickfergus
Chas. Robb	"	Thomas Blair	"
Francis Crossen	"	John Michael	Washington City
James C. Mulligan	Banbridge	George Barr	Aughnacloy
James Gilmore	Co. Tyrone	William Barr	"
Edward M'Evoy	"	Margaret Barr	"
Robt. M'Kean	"	William Baxter	"
David Wilson	"	James Hardy	"
Joseph Wilson	"	Mary Hardy	"
Mary Wilson	"	Jane Hardy	"
James Wilson	"	Mary Hardy	"
Andrew Martin	Co. Antrim	Margaret Hardy	"
Robert Steen	"	James Hardy	"
Archibald Waters	"	George Hardy	"
Hugh Smith	"	Andrew Gordon	Newtownards
William Carroll	"	G. M'Laughlin	Co. Tyrone
Margaret Monderson	"	James Kyle	"
Sarah Monderson	"	A. Ballentine	"
Isaac Monderson	"	S. Reid	"
John Monderson	"	L. M'Linchy	"
John Ennis	Belfast	G. W. Nicholl	"
James Hagen	"	John Anderson	Castlereagh

16-46

(a) Brig Boudain, from Newry, arrived at New York on August 1, 1816.

(c)

Robert Laughton	Laughgall	Sarah Cumming	Co. Down
Elizabeth James	Castle Caufield	Eliza Anne Cumming	"
Robert Alexander	Co. Armagh	Sarah Cumming	"
Margaret Alexander	"	William Cumming	"
George Alexander	"	Chambers Cumming	"
Anne Jane Alexander	"	Thomas M'Lawry	"
Harriet Alexander	"	James Conn	"
Mary Small Alexander	"	Hugh Minnis	"
* Hugh Small Alexander	"	James Haffey	Newry
James Claughey	"	Michael Handfield	Co. Cavan
Mary Claughey	"	William O'Donnel	Co. Monaghan
* John Claughey	"	James Hogans	"
* Sarah Claughey	"	Esther Hogans	"
---- Claughey	"	* John Hogans	"
Thomas Alexander	"	* Mary Hogans	"
Jane Alexander	"	John Largey	"
Samuel Lowry	Co. Tyrone	James Cauley	Co. Meath
Thomas Lowry	"	Thomas Cauley	"
Thomas Cumming	North Carloina	* Children.	

6-47

(a) Brig John, from Galway, arrived at New York on August 2, 1816.

(c)

Peter Kilfoyle	Parish of Kildare, King's Co.
John Duffy	"
Martin Daly	"
Samuel Flanagan	"
William Gannon	"
Michael Daly	"
Ellen Daly	"
Michael Lally	Buttersbridge, Co. Cavan
John Lilly	"
Patrick Cannoughton	Longford
Michael Toole	Tram, Co. Galway
Michael Burke	Ballina, Co. Mayo
William Daly	"
William Rider	Aghram, Co. Galway
David Dillan	Ballywaslee, Co. Galway
Darby Hardman	Tyapien, Co. Galway
Dennis Ganner	Asker, Co. Galway
Patrick Nanghten	Athlone, Co. Westmeath
John Dannan	"
Robert Cannon	"
Bridget Cannon	"
Anne Farrel	"
John Raftrey	"
Hugh Brady	Currefin, Co. Galway
Thomas Graham	Ballyfair, Co. Kildare
Mary Graham	"
Charles Daily	Coldaragh
James McLaughlin	Somerset, Co. Galway
John McLaughlin	"
Patrick Niven	"
Edward Hynes	Melick, Co. Galway
Andrew Fahy	Leitrim
Cornelius Cavey	Curreigh, Co. Galway
James Thompson	Stonepark, Co. Roscommon
William Lambert	Lambert-Ledge, Co. Galway
John Regin	St. Nicholas, Galway
Henry Kerwan	"
Francis Burke	"
Patrick Reddington	Longhrea, Co. Galway
Patrick D. Arcy	Ballinrobe

16-48

(a) Ship Ontario, from Dublin, arrived at New York on August 7, 1816.

(c)
Anne Boyce	Wexford	Anne Keating	
Mary Anne Lane	Almeritia	and child	Kilkenny
Catherine Davenport	Dublin	John Morine	"
Grace Rudd	"	Judith Morine	
John Wass	"	and two children	"
Catherine Dempsey	"	Bryan Daly	"
Jane Branick		Ellen Daly and	
and child	"	three children	"
Edward Farrel	"	Margaret Price	
John Kenedy	"	and 3 children	"
Bridget Kenedy	"	Less M'Daniel	"
Thomas Ingraham, wife		Owen M'Daniel	"
and 9 children	"	Ellen Parcell	
Bryan M'Carthy	Cavan	and child	"
Fanny Armstrong		Bridget Brennan	"
and 4 children	"	Mary Mulhall	"
Joseph Long	"	James Irwin	Coothill
James Brown	"	Patrick Cusack	"
Bridget Gregory		Mary Ryan & child	Carlow
and two children	Mead	Margaret Ryan	"
Anne Daren	"	Michael Kelly	"
Catharine Sweetman	"	Mary Kelly	"
Mary Greenham	"	Daniel Keenan	Upperwood
Thomas Castigan	"	Laurence Harkin	Kildare
Thomas Keenan	"	Mary Harkin	
Ellen Keenan		and 3 children	"
and child	"	John Lockwood	Leister
John M'Dermot	"	William Priston	"
Mathew Salman	"	Daniel Bergin	Queen's Co.
Patrick M'Cormick	Leitrim	William Faley	"
Esther M'Cormick	"	James M'Donel	"
Robert Kane	"	John Murtaugh	Westmeath
Michael Pendergrass	Kilkenny	Bridget Robins	
Patrick Breman	"	and child	"
Ellen Bremen		Michael Mathews	Drogheda
and two children	"	John Howell	Landaff
Edward Keating	"	James M'Connell	Monaghan

16-49

(a) Brig Margaret, from Sligo, arrived at New York on August 8, 1816.

(c)
Robert Henderson
Sibby Burk
Peter Smith
Charles Poany
Catherine Roney
Anne Roaney
James Michaw
Henry D. Neill
Madge D. Neill
Anne Ward
Patrick Ward
Owen McMarrow
Mary McMarrow
Mary Haran
Charles Kilmartin
Martin Queenan
Michael Curry
Margaret Branely

James Gunigle
Owen Gillown
Anne Gillown
Michael Fuman
Mary Connelly
Bryan Folin
Mary Falin
Edward Earrie
Andrew McHugh
Samuel Henry
Anne Henry
* James W. Henry
John Gillen
Patrick Eagan
James White
William Trotter
Margaret Healy

Daniel Fioheley
Bernard McManns
Charles Brainerd
Jane Wilson
Martin Rosman
Martin Hill
Allen Cullen
John Hay
Daniel Richley
Dennis McPhilown
John Castello
J. Discord
Martin Feeney
Thos. McDonald
Jane Allen
William Fallan
Elizabeth Mochan
* Children.

16-50

(a) Brig Mount-Bay, from Londonderry, arrived at New York on August 12, 1816.

(c)
Henry M'Veigh	Tyrone
John Coulter	"
Malcolm Leech	"
Hugh Wardler	"
William Stuart	"
Jos. Cook	"
Archibald Johnston	"
A. Leech	"
Margaret M'Philaney	"
Patrick M'Gum	"
Philip McSwigan	"
Mary McSwigan	"
John Doogan	"
John Camble	"
Samuel Johnston	"
James McSerley	"
James McVaid	"
Andrew Sheran	"
Robert Botham	"
Terence McCusker	"
Isabella Botham	"
Francis McNemee	"
P. Daly	"
Bernard Ganway	"

Hugh Gorman	Tyrone
Wm. McNama	"
George Hartness	"
Neil Clark	"
John McKeown, senr.	"
Samuel McKeown	"
Mary McKeown	"
Sarah McKeown	"
Saml. McKeown	"
* Margaret McKeown	"
* Anne McKeown	"
William McKeown	"
John McKeown junr.	"
William Causland	"
Catherine McGlyn	"
Dennis McGowan	"
Henry Daily	"
Patrick McGreevy	"
Robert Crosby	"
Andrew Craig	"
Mathew White	"
Robert Eager	"
William Forbes, senr.	"
Jane Forbes	"

William Forbes junr.	Tyrone	Robert McGuragle	Londonderry
John Forbes	"	William Stuart	"
Fanny Forbes	"	William Walker	"
John Davies	"	John Bell	"
William Richie	"	Bryan Hassen	"
Catherine Richie	"	James McCallan	"
Bernard Gormley	"	Patrick Hutton	"
Armour Spraule	"	James Hutton	"
Robert Carmachy	"	Thomas Carabine	"
Mary McCanaghy	"	Catherine Carabine	"
David McCanaghy	"	William Carmeran	"
Alexander White	"	Elizabeth Carmeran	"
Elizabeth White	"	Allen Carmeran	"
Ellen White	"	Anne Carmeran	"
Rose McGinn	"	Alexander Bond	"
Mary McKeown junr.	"	Patrick Carlan	"
Christopher Paisley	Londonderry	Sarah Carlan	"
Robert Cochran	"	James Jackson	"
William Segarson	"	John Worrhington	"
Robert Semple	"	Susan Young	"
William Sithgon	"	Maria Doherty	"
William Brawley senr.	"	Hugh Cooke	"
* William Brawley jr.	"	David Cooke	"
Isabella Brawley	"	William Lighton	"
Samuel Mitchell	"	John Hassan	"
Sohn Boke	"	Alexander Hassan	"
William Hargon	"	Joseph Arthur	Antrim
William Johnson	"	Rebecca Arthur	"
James Hunter	"	Thomas Robinson	"
Mary Hunter	"	Anthony McAlister	"
William Anderson	"	John Quinn	Donegal
Eliza Anderson	"	Charles Quinn	"
James Crawford	"	James Chls. Green	"
John Crawford	"	John McMenomy	"
Mary McLaughlin	"	Daniel McComb	"
William Hunter	"	Francis Quinn	"
John Kane	"	James Quinn	"
John Henderson	"	James McCool	"
John Rosborough	"	William Sharkey	"
John Aiken	"	* Children.	

16-51

(a) Brig Barkley, from Londonderry, arrived at New York on August 14, 1816.

(c)

Name	Place		Name	Place
George Buchan	Rambleton		* Mary Chambers	Danaghdee
Neile M'Cloud	Londonderry		* Margaret Chambers	"
Anne M'Cloud	"		* Robert Chambers	"
Daniel M'Cloud	"		* William Chambers	"
* John M'Cloud	"		Sarah Chambers	"
* James M'Cloud	"		John M'Crossin	"
* Mary Anne M'Cloud	"		William M'Intosh	"
John Pollock	"		Jane M'Intosh	"
Wm. Deulin	"		Alexander Keer	Newtown Stuart
James Ferguson	"		John Black	Rathlin
John Miller	"		John M'Dangall	Letterkenny
Patrick Cassell	Armagh		William M'Menomy	"
Robert Covenagh	Dannegall		Elizabeth M'Menomy	"
Clark Mathewson	Strabane		* Thomas M'Menomy	"
David Mathewson	"		* Robt. M'Menomy	"
Peter Coling	Morrill		* Elizabeth M'Menomy	"
Patrick German	"		Mary M'Dangal	"
Mary Gorman	"		Hugh M'Menomy	"
* Hugh Gorman	"		James Mitchel	"
James Watt	Templemore		Robert M'Ilheny	"
Dennis McLaughlin	----		James Galsngher	"
Andrew Leech	Balbrigan		Edward Moffat	"
Sarah Leech	"		Maney Scanlon	"
Robert Chambers	Danaghdee		John Mulheron	Caldatt
Margaret Chambers	"		Ralph Danford	"
James Chambers	"		James Danford	"
Mathew Chambers	"		John Campbell	Enniskillen
Agnes Chambers	"		Robert Smyth	"
Eliza Chambers	"		* Children.	

111

16-52

(a) Brig Juno, from Sligo, landed in New London; passengers transferred to
the sloop MacDonough and arrived at New York on August 16, 1816.

(c)
John Gibbs	Co. Cavan	Patrick McAnalty	Sligo
James Wright	Newtown Stewart	Peter Lynch	"
Bryan Scinlon	Castleton	Felix Murry	"
Hugh Hart	Grange	Andrew Pigeon	"
James Stevens	Sligo	Martin Mitchell	"
Samuel Henry	"	Michael Gorvarn	"
John Henry	"	Charles Roony	"
David Henry	"	Jane Wright	"
Samuel Henry	"	John Wright	"
George Henry	"	Mariam Wright	"
John Keeny	"	Bridget Murray	"
James McDonagh	"	Catherine Jones	"
Roger Janes	"	Ruth Gibbs	"
William Janes	"	Mary Gibbs	"
Hugh Hart	"	John Gibbs	"
John Hoy	"	Patrick Travers	Lurganboy
Bryan Scandler	"	James Mara	"
Andrew McGown	"		

16-53

(a) Ship Bristol, from Dublin, arrived at New York on December 14, 1816.

(c)
Thomas Gordon	Co. Cavan	* Catharine Conry	Kilkenny
Alexander Pogue	"	Margaret Lambert	"
Patrick Caselly	Armagh	Edward M'Laughlin	"
Philip Laphen	"	Dennis Rafter	"
Michael M'Donnell	Thurles	Mary Clear	"
Judith M'Donnell	"	Dennis Tracy	"
Margaret M'Donnell	"	* Mary Tracy	"
John Phelan	Queen's Co.	* Catharine Tracy	"
James Moore	Dublin	Thomas Tracy	"
James Costigan	"	Michael Dowling	"
Thomas Benningham	"	John Dwyer	"
Eliza Benningham	"	Thomas Maxwell	"
John Stephens	"	Robert Clancy	Athlone
John Linnan	"	Isaac Carr	Waterford
William James Farrell	"	Bernard Pettit	Co. Longford
Mary Duffy		Joseph Glynn	Co. Tipperary
and child	Carrickmacross	Thomas James	New York
Michael Conry	Kilkenny	Maria Briggs	"
Judith Conry	"	James Johnson	Nr. Sheffield
* Mary Conry	"	Samuel Johnson	"
		* Children.	

112

(a) Ship Neptune, from Belfast, arrived at New York on January 10, 1817.

(c)
Wm. Brown	Armagh	Hugh Gordon	Tyrone
James Powe	"	Margaret Ban *	Derry
Robert Caldwell	"	George Ban *	"
John Scowels	"	Jane Ban	"
Joseph Leggit	"	James Potts	Down
Wm. Keys	"	Ann Potts	"
Wm. Simmons	"	Ann Potts junr.	"
John Hagan	"	Robert Potts *	"
Arthur M'Ginnis	Belfast	Josiah Beaty	"
Thomas Johnston	"	Wm. Beaty	"
James Graham	"	Jane Beaty	"
John Maher	"	Arine Beck	"
Elizabeth Maher	"	Joseph Currin	"
Wm. Smith	Tyrone	Eliza Currin *	"
George Ban	"	James Corbit	Dublin
George Elliott	"	Wm. Rochfort	"
		* Children.	

(a) Ship Rose in Bloom, from Belfast, arrived at New York on January 15, 1817.

(c)
John Barton   Armagh
Sarah Dunlevy   "
Mary Montgomery, Castleblaney,
James Smith   "   , Co. Monaghan
James Johnston, Drumcrie, Co. Armagh
Samuel Ceery, K---gally, Co. Armagh
Mary Geery,   "   "
Andrew Sheils, Clones, Co. Monaghan
Stuart McKee, Loughbrickland,
                          Co. Down
Adam Rutherford, Ballynahinch, "
James Black, Glas--gh, Co. Monaghan
Margaret Black   "   "
Andrew Wiggins, Ballygawley,
John Wiggins,   "   , Co. Armagh
Eliza Wiggins,   "   "

Margaret Wiggins, Ballygawley, Co. Armagh
* John Wiggins jr.   "   "
* Hugh Wiggins   "   "
Thomas McCartney   "   "
George McDowel   "   "
Charles McGivern, Laughgall, Co. Armagh
John Reid, Tanderagee, Co. Armagh
Mary Reid
James Dowling   Kildare
Thomas Dowling   "
William Bailie jr. New York
John Booth   England
John Smith   "
Richard Stock   "
Sarah Stock   "
* Children.

17-3

(a) Ship Anne Alexander, from Dublin, arrived at New York on February 22, 1817

(c)
Alexander Steele	Dublin	John Church	Dublin
Peter Duff	"	George Toule	Co. Wicklow
Michael Kelly	"	Garrit Kelly	"
Patrick Troy	"	Lawrence Power	Co. Carlow
Francis Moore	"	John Barton	Halifax
James Allen	"		

17-4

(a) Brig Calypso, from Dublin, arrived at New York on March 12, 1817.

(c)
Edward McShane	Dublin	William Beadle	United States	
Michael Failling	"	William Beadle junr.	"	"
John Gardner	"	John Beadle	"	"
Thomas Patterson		Luke Usher		
and family	England	and daughter	"	"
Robert Ward		---- Wallace	New York	
and wife	----			

17-5

(a) Ship Columbus, from Liverpool, arrived at New York on March 12, 1817.

(c) Ignatius McDonough, Heapstown, Co. Sligo, Ireland

17-6

(a) Ship Loyal Sam, from Sligo, arrived at New York on March 27, 1817.

(c)
Owen Morris	Sligo	Bridget McCawl	Sligo
Mary Morris	"	Thomas Reilly	"
* W. Morris	"	+ Edward Dugan	New York
* Sarah Morris	"	+ Joseph Rodgers	"
* John Morris	"	John McKean	Scotland
Hugh McCawl	"	* Children.	
Anne McCawl	"	+ U.S. Citizens.	

(a) Ship Dublin Packet, from Dublin, arrived at New York on May 1, 1817.

(c)

Robert McLentock	Dublin	Hugh Materson	Dublin
George Teeling	"	Margaret Matterson	"
Mrs. Dillon	"	Felix Geoffrey	"
Charles Jones	"	Jane Dempsey	"
Guy Coclough	"	John Clark	"
James Arnold	"	Robert Kenny	"
William Brown	"	Margaret Kenny	"
Richard Brett	"	* James Kenny	"
Maria Sharp	"	* Gregory Kenny	"
* George Sharp	"	* Mary Kenny	"
Catherine Reed	"	* Ellen Kenny	"
* Elizabeth Reed	"	Catherine Kelly	"
Mary Smith	"	William Gent	"
Robt. Cunningham	"	Patrick O'Donnell	"
William Reed	"	+ Thomas Hunter	New Jersey
Margaret Smith	"	+ Richard Hunter	"
* George Smith	"	Charles Cumming	Scotland
* Andrew Smith	"		
Mary Smith	"	* Children.	
Mary Ann Cunningham	"	+ U.S. Citizens.	

(a) Brig Anne, Captain Scott, from Dublin, arrived at New York on May 5, 1817.

(b) Commendation of Captain Scott signed by:

John McDonnell   Rowland Reynolds
Richard Salmon   William Grattan
Samuel Cunningham   William Doyle
Patrick Hanley

(c)

William Doyle	Dublin	Samuel Cunningham	Dublin
William Grattan	"	Richard Connell	"
Benjamin P. Binns	"	Anthony Kennedy	"
John Binns	"	John Cuthbert	"
* Richard Salmon	"	Deborah Cuthbert	"
John Beahan	"	* John Cuthbert	"
Maria Hamilton	"	Michael Clare	"
Margaret Hamilton	"	John Cox	"
* Eliza Hamilton	"	James Ryan	"
Wm. Pigot	"	Henry Grey	"
David Dyas	"	John McDonnel	Co. Wicklow
William Freeman	"	Edward Dowser	"
Thomas Dempsey	"	Patrick Carolan	Newry
Christopher Murphy	"	Rowland Reynolds	N. York.
Philip Grace	"		
Patrick Hanly	"	* Children.	

(a) Brig Ann, from Belfast, arrived at New York on May 13, 1817.

(c)

John Sheridan	Monaghan	David Thompson	Belfast
Patrick Hughs	"	Robert McCrea	"
Francis Brady	"	Bernard O'Hare	"
Moses Cochran	Dromore	Joseph Berry	"
Anne Cochran	"	John Whiteford	"
Thom. Cochran	"	Hugh M-u-any	"
William Cochran	"	Thomas Phillips	Ballymena
Samuel Cochran	"	Jane Phillips	"
Joseph Cochran	"	Grace Phillips	"
James Wallace	Coleraine	John Hamilton	Bushmills
John Willis	Dungannon	Walter Hall	Armagh
Robert Orr	Belfast	Thomas McCullough	----
David Shaw	"		

(a) Ship Ontario, from Dublin, arrived at New York on May 16, 1817.

(c)

+ James Moffatt		Mary Read	
and wife	Dublin	and 3 children	Drogheda
+ Charles Reade	"	Bridget Yore	"
+ Mrs. Dixon		Michael Magrah	"
and child	Dublin	Andrew Magrah	"
Jared Irwin, wife		John Gregory	"
and children	Dublin	Anne Mathews	"
Peter Doerty	"	Thomas Morris	Co. Westmeath
James Casey	"	Michael Keenan	Co. Meath
John Cunningham	"	Francis Keenan	"
Mary Cunningham		Patrick Monk	"
and child	Dublin	Mathew Crosby	"
James Stewart	Armagh	Owen Martagh	"
Martin McMahon	Queen's Co.	John Maguire	Co. Tipperary
John Kennedy	"	Charles Mitchell	Cavan
Patrick Quirk	"	Robt. Johnson	"
Patrick Dempsey	"	William Jackson	"
John Dough	"	William Killen	King's Co.
Elizabeth Dough	"	Christopher Fell	London
+ Richard Lee	"	John Collins	Lancashire, Engl
Anne Doolin	"	Robert Featon	"
Michael Brennan	"	Edward Featan	"
Margaret Yore		James Garnett	"
and 3 children	Drogheda	+ U.S. Citizens.	

17-11

(a) Ship Neptune, from Dublin, arrived at New York on May 24, 1817.

(c)
Thomas Hogan	Dublin	* Bridget Collins	Roscommon
John Pierpoint	"	Eleanor Collins	"
Alex. Campbell	"	* Patrick Collins	"
Mary Knaggs	"	* William Collins	"
Wm. Callaghan	"	William Houghton	Limerick
Owen Divine	"	Philip Karney	Wicklow
James Kiegan	"	John Byrue	"
Nicholas Murphy	"	Eliza Byrne	"
Mary Murphy	"	Anne Byrne	"
* Thomas Murphy	"	Mary Wild	New York
* John Murphy	"	A. Dobbs	Canada
Edward Jones	"	Mrs. Dobbs	"
Elizabeth Jones	"	Thomas Cartwright	"
John Denit	"	Mary Moony	"
Rich. Wright	"	Edward O'Hara	"
Hugh Collins	Roscommon		
Mary Collins	"	* Children.	

17-12

(a) Brig Frances, from Sligo, arrived at New York on May 25, 1817.

(c)
Stephen Hilliken	New York
John B. Javison	England

(a) Ship Commodore Perry, from Sligo, arrived at New York on May 26, 1817.

(c)

Jane Gardner	Edenreigh	James Murphy	Killeshandra
Margaret Kennedy	Newton	Eliza McCormick	Carrick
Timothy Kennedy	"	Esther McCormick	"
Sibby Hoy	Crevagh	Bridget McTernan	Killaregy
Luke Gilmartin	Drumfad	Peter Golden	Wynesforth
Mary Gilmartin		Catharine McGowan	Geograth
Bridget Cullen	Grange	Henry Dalton	Sligo
Michael Curnin	Darlchan	Catherine McGuire	"
William Curnin	Ballintrellah	Bernard Feilly	Ballynamore
Edward Kilkenny	Glebe	Patrick Kearns	Kildrogy
Thomas McElroy	Lurganboy	John Cullen	Grange
Bridget McElroy	"	Patrick McGowan	----
Hugh O'Donnel	Dranbady	Andrew McGowan	
Daniel O'Donnel	"	Daniel Gardner	
William Mecham	Bunduff	Michael McGowan	
Barbary Mecham	"	Daniel McGowan	
James Mecham	"	Catherine Gillespy	
Eleanor Healy	Moneygold	B. West	
Judith Healy	"	Dolly Clinton	
Catharine Finlay	Grange	Margaret McGloin	
William Rooney	Tully	Bridget McGloin	
James Clinton	Crevymore	Michael McGowan	
Barbara McGowen	Annah	* Mary McTernan	
Martin Smyth	Condry	* William McGowan	
Bridget Rooney, sen.	"	* Hannah Clinton	
Bridget Rooney junr.	"	* Children.	

(a) Ship Westpoint, from Belfast, arrived at New York on May 29, 1817.

(b) Had been advertised to sail from Belfast on April 1.

(c)

Eleanor Montgomery	Belfast	Michael Gafney	Ballimena
Jane Montgomery	"	Mary Law	Antrim
Margaret Montgomery	"	English Crawford	"
Jane Harrison	"	Jane Crawford	"
George Bell	"	James Crawford	"
Dennis Doyle	Breanbridge	John Crawford	"
William Clark	Lisburn	John Jones	"
Mary Clark	"	Thomas Innis	Saintfield
Robert Clark	"	David Shaw	"
Thomas Wilson	"	Philip Kelly	"
Charles Tollis	Ballimena	W. Gaffney	"
Rose Tollis	"	John Dunegan	"
John Burns	"	Sarah Phillips	Clough
I. Burns	"	Catherine Phillips	"
Anne Burns	"	James Ellis	Donegan
Judith Burns	"	James Quinn	Dungannan
Thomas Burns	"	Charles Quinn	"
Bridget Smith	"	Clement Burlugh	Pennsylvania
Anne Fitch	"	Thomas Stevenson	Philadelphia
John Burn	"	John Watson	New York
Deven Murray	"	Alexander Francis	Bangor
Felix Murray	"	Thomas Chamber	"
Mary Murray	"	Letitia Chamber	"
Philip Brady	"	Thomas Tate	Albany

17-15

(a) Ship Hibernia, from Londonderry, arrived at New York on June 1, 1817.

(c)

David Crocket	Edinmore	* John Young	Antrim
Alexander McKeever	Castlefin	* Eliza Young	"
Robert McKeever	"	Margaret Blythe	"
Susannah McGowan	"	Jane Armstrong	"
* John McGowan	"	Catherine Colligan	"
* Ferral McGowan	"	Susan McGeehan	Raphoe
John Moore	Fermanagh	* Catherine McGeehan	"
Alice Moore	"	* Susan McGeehan	"
* Grace Moore	"	George Neelis	"
James Sharpe	"	Margaret Neelis	"
Jane Sharpe	"	Hugh Hannagan	Strabane
* Mary Sharpe	"	Gowan Martin	"
* John Sharpe	"	Wm. Doherty	"
Francis Quinn	"	Charles Gallagher	Culduff
Margaret Quinn	"	Patrick Haviland	Londonderry
William Young	Antrim	Elizabeth Bailey	"
Keziah Young	"	* Robert Bailey	"

17-15 (c), continued

* Moses Bailey	Londonderry	James Bradley	Letkenny
Samuel Ewing	"	James McGinnis	Greencastle
John Rutledge	Irvinstown	Forest Reid	Ramelton
Alice Rutledge	"	Henry Carrigan	Enniskillen
Mary Graham	"	Martin Morrison	"
* Joseph Graham	"	Robert Shuran	Dungiven
* Mary Graham	"	Robert Nelson	Drumcannon
Patrick Colligan	Letkenny	* Children.	

17-16

(a) Ship Anne, from Cork, arrived at New York on June 3, 1817.

(c) Mary Keating	Youghall	David Hurley	Cove
* Margaret Keating	"	James Kelly	Mallow
Maria Keating	"	Francis Warham	"
* Elizabeth Keating	"	Patrick Mape	Ballybay
William Kirby	"	Francis Mape	"
John Supple	Cork	Nicholas Quirk	Killarney
Patrick Driscole	"	John Harrington	----
Timothy Cotton	Bantry		
Thomas McGuire	Cove	* Children.	

17-17

(a) Brig Hugh Wallace, from Belfast, arrived at Norfolk before June 7, 1817.

(b) Had been advertised to sail from Belfast on April 5.

(c) Robert Robinson	Mary Ellis senr.	James M'Cartin
John Murray	Mary Ellis junr.	Francis Taylor
Dr. Robert Murray	Jane Ellis	Mary Taylor
Samuel Riddle	John Ellis	and infant
Francis Devitt	Robert Nickson	James Blackely
Frances Patkinson	George Lyons	John Lenox
Francis Bailey	James M'Naughton	James Robinson
Alexander Gibson	David Sloan	Thomas Coleman
John Killen	Andrew Boyd	Robert Patterson
Mary Killen	Hugh Boyle	William Magill
and infant	Maxwell Drennan	Wm. Scott
Hugh Killen	Samuel Hunter	Robert Ferguson
Wm. Rodgers	John Hunter	Robert Johnston
Wm. Ellis	Sarah Hunter	Hugh Kennedy
Rebecca Ellis senr.	Mary Hunter	James Henderson
Rebecca Ellis junr.	Margaret M'Mullen	

(a) Brig Tiffin, from Dublin, arrived at New York on June 6, 1817.

(c)

James Finigan	Dublin	---- Couy	Dublin
Michael Conly	"	Henry McEnally	"
Margaret Conly	"	Catherine Caher	
Patrick McKenna	"	and child	"
James Murphy	"	Elizabeth Caffer	"
Terence McDermott	"	Edw. Pumall (?)	Wales
Patrick Trenor	"	Benj. James	"
Patrick Kernan	"	John ----	England
Edward McNenagh	"	George Morehouse	"
Mary Sherry	"	John Hardgraves	"
James Couy	"	Lavina Morehouse	"

17-19

(a) Ship Victory, from Limerick in 35 days, arrived at New Bedford on June 11, 1817.

(b) The passengers, one excepted, arrived in New York before June 28 and intended to proceed to Ohio.

(c)

Nathaniel Wakefield	Ballisneloe	William Hickson,	
Robert Wakefield	"	wife & 2 children	Tralee
Francis Wakefield		Thomas Howard	
and child	"	and wife	Co. Tipperary
John Mossop, wife		William Hayes	Cahir
and 2 children	Burrisakane	Henry Moore	Limerick
Thomas Hobs, wife			
and child	Burrisakane	"There were also two ladies from	
Thomas Casey	Co. Limerick	Limerick, whose names I did not	
Jeremiah Dempsey	"	learn."	
Edward Hickson			
and two sons	Tralee		

17-20

(a) Ship Aeolus, from Londonderry, arrived at New York on June 18, 1817.

(c)
William Kelly	Esther Caldwell	Denis Dougherty
Adam Smyth	Alexander Caldwell	James Lindsay
James Smyth	* James Caldwell	James Moore
Robert Henderson	* Mary Caldwell	Sally Moore
Martha Robinson	* Tho. Caldwell	Anthony Carney
* Mary Porter	Catherine Johnson	* John Carney
* Charles Robinson	James Sheskeron	William Boyle
* Andrew Robinson	William Kyle	James Cuthbertson
* James Robinson	Andrew McKinley	William Smyth
* Stewart Robinson	Alexander McKinley	Margaret Moore
* Roberts Robinson	Jane McKinley	Robert Moore
William McCally	* Robert Lowrey	George McGowan
Mary Caldwell	* Susan Lowrey	* Children.

17-21

(a) Brig Factor, from Newry, arrived at New York on June 20, 1817.

(c)
James Scott	James Tole	Eliza Boyle
James Doran	John Tole	George Barton
Eliza & Jane Giedhill	James Murphy	John Barton
Thomas Curran	Patrick King	James Burke
John Doran	John Larkin	Anne M'Cullough
Richard Marmian	Edward Mooney	Hugh M'Cullough
James Hamilton	James McKeoun	Mary Fegan
Eliza. Hamilton	Hugh McKeoun	Frances Fegan
Sarah Kearns	Catharine McKeoun	Margaret Fegan
Jane Kearns	Patrick Murphy	Rosetta Fegan
John Kearns	John Young	Felix McCave
Rosetta Kearns	Abraham Booth	Margaret McKinney
William Kearns	Henry Howth	Thomas Miers
John Kelly	James Fearly	George Young
Catharine Kelly	Charles Caberty	Charles Dowlin
	Catharine Caberty	Rose Kelly

17-22

(a) Ship Foster, from Belfast, arrived at New York on July 5, 1817.

(b) Had been advertised to sail from Belfast on March 16.

(c)
J. W. Wright	Eliza McKay	William Hutcheson
Eliza Wright	Mary Kennedy	Patrick McCanna
* Richard Wright	Samuel Boden	Anne McCanna
* Eliza Wright	Elizabeth Boden	Ellen McCanna
* John Wright	William Boden	Robt. McCullough
* George Wright	Samuel Boden	Alexander McQuoid
William Sharp	Matilda Boden	* Margaret McBride
P. McCambridge	John McFerran	Samuel Cameron
* Robert Lowry	James Toole	Wm. Dermont
William McRride	Jane Toole	Agnes Dermont
William Dermont	Margaret Ferguson	Adam Graham
Isabella Dermont	* James Ferguson	Patrick McGuire
David Law	Robert Sloan	Bernard Byrnes
Kezia Law	Elizabeth Sloan	Catherine Byrnes
* I. Law	Hamilton Clark	S. Byrnes
* Mary Law	Peter Hagan	M. Byrnes
* Margaret Law	Dennis Hagan	H. Byrnes
* L. Law	Jane Hutcheson	John McMillan
Grace Hillies	David Barclay	James Patton
		* Children.

17-23

(a) Ship Down, from Belfast, arrived at New York on July 9, 1817.

(c)
James Robertson	Robert Service	* Mary Farrell
Margaret Kennedy	William Shields	John Holiday
* James Kennedy	Mary Shields	Robert Young
* William Kennedy	* Robert Shields	George McClelland
* Susannah Kennedy	Robert Park	James Walker
Jesse Horp	Robert Dunlap	James Ritchie
James Horp	Anne Dunlap	Roger Judge
* Mary Horp	* Jno. Dunlap	Phillip Judge
* Margaret Horp	Mary Dunlap	Charles Ward
James Booth	* Margaret Dunlap	James Seeds
Jonathan Spite	* Eliza J. Dunlap	M. Seeds
Richard Wright	* Robert Dunlap	Hugh Coruie
Peter Brown	Wm. Arthur	Jane Thompson
Catherine Brown	Mathew Smith	* Jane Thompson
* William Brown	John R. Smith	James Sterling
* Jane Brown	Charles McCaliman	Kennedy Glenvie
Andrew Bailie	George Farrel	Henry Delaqutus
William Steele	Mary Farrell	James Henery
John Marshall	* Susannah Farrell	James McIrish
William Dobbin	George Farrell	* Children.

(a) Ship Bristol, from Newry, arrived at New York on July 12, 1817.

(b) James McBride, aged 29 years, a native of Rathfriland, died on board the Bristol.

(c)

David Martin	Belfast	George Rea	Newry
Robert Martin	"	Elizabeth Brady	Redhills
Anne Morehead	Laughbrickland	James Blean	Co. Meath
Anne Nesbit	"	Elizabeth Blean	"
Samuel McRee	"	Wm. Blean	"
Elizabeth Reddick	Co. Down	John Blean	"
F. Reddick	"	George Blean	"
* N. Reddick	"	Anne Blean	"
* J. Reddick	"	Rose Anne Blean	"
* A. Reddick	"	Robert Burrows	Armagh
John Magee	Rathfriland	Eliza Burrows	"
Mary Magee	"	James McBride Burrows	"
George McClory	"	Edward Thompson	"
William Moffat	"	Michael McCartney	Co. Louth
William Moffat junr.	"	William Cogbran	Derry
Mathew McBride	"	Andrew C. Brown	Co. Cavan
Hans McBride	"	Patrick Henry	Fauhhart
Wm. Little	"	Richard Evans	Dundalk
John Little	"	William Donavin	Warrenspoint
Francis Quinn	Keady	Samuel Lindsay	Dromore
Catherine Quinn	"	Anne Lindsay	"
Mary Fegan	"	* Children.	

(a) Schooner Vigilant, from Belfast, arrived at New York on July 21, 1817.

(c)

Charles Wilson	Belfast
James Mathews	"
Francis Phillips	"

(a) Brig Britannia, from Newry, arrived at New York on July 22, 1817.

(c)

James Skeffington	Newry	Jane M'Connell	Banbridge
William Cowan	"	John M'Cabe	Co. Cavan
Sarah Cowan	"	Catherine M'Cabe	"
William Cowden		James Miller	"
William Cowden jr.		Sally Miller	"
David Cowden		Luke Babe	Dramore
Anne Cowden		John Short	Loughbrickland
Jane Lankey	Dungannon	Roger McPoland	"
William Saunderson	"	Eleanor McPoland	"
James Saunderson	"	John Dallas	"
Robert Saunderson	"	Patrick McLoughlin	Forkhilt
Robert McTier	"	Bernard Varley	
John M'Connell	Banbridge	James Murphy	

17-27

(a) Ship Calpe, from Dublin, arrived at New York on July 28, 1817.

(c)

Patrick Henrick	Dublin	James Sullivan	Co. Louth
Michael Avery	"	Daniel Coyle	Donegal
Bernard M'Cann	Co. Cavan	Patrick Coyle	"
Mrs. M'Cann	"	Catherine Coyle	"
Patrick Gallagher	"	Catherine Murray	"
Jane Farrel	"	+ John Coyle	"
Michael Cunningham	"	Alicia Byrne	"
Nicholas Trevan	"	Peter Mearse	"
Elizabeth Trevan	"	Anthony Keenan	Co. Fermanagh
John Cunningham	Drogheda	Terence Keenan	"
Mrs. Cunningham	"	Terence M'Caffrey	"
* Margaret Cunningham	"	+ Alfred Hynes	Co. Mayo
* John Cunningham	"	+ James M'Gowan	Baltimore
Matthew Dogherty	Co. Louth	+ Jacob Ricketts	New York
Margaret Dogherty	"	* Children.	
Peter Cassidy	"	+ U.S. Citizens.	

17-28

(a) Brig Agnes, from Waterford, arrived at New York on August 9, 1817.

(c)

John Griffith	Waterford	Matthew Pierce	Wexford
Samuel Cottom	"	William Furlong	"
Pearse Perden	"	Richard Keating	Dublin
William Braydon		Michael Kelly	"
and wife	"	John Finnigan	"
Philip Furlong	"	Mary White	Ross
John Cowman	"	James Handlen	Clonmel
George Hedderington	"	Peter Warren	Cárrick
William Sparrow	"	Richard Murphy	"
Robert Murphy	"	Nathaniel Davis	Carlow
John Murphy	"	Hugh Dempsey	"
Richard Rice	"	* George Davis	"
Godfrey Kennedy	"	* Thomas Davis	"
Dennis Brady	"	Michael Carroll	"
Daniel Halligan	"	Michael Doolen	"
Bridget Halligan	"	Miss Gough	Wexford
George Walsh	"	Bridget Walsh	"
David Murphy	"	Edward Murphy	Waterford
Robert Dudley	"	James Hannsberry	"
Patrick Culliton	"	George Morrison	"
Dennis Murphy	Wexford	Peter Connoly	"
Nicholas Power	"	Mrs. Mahers & child	"
Richard Devereaux	"	Jeremiah Doherty	"
Martin Fortune	"	James Reddy	"
		* Children.	

17-29

(a) Ship Erin, from Dublin, arrived at New York on August 13, 1817.

(c)

Edward Kavanah	William Sweeny	Thomas Ennis
Patrick Brady	Philip Dignan	John M'Nally
Patrick Brady junr.	Richard Barclay	Patrick Callon
Bridget Brady	Richard Atkinson	William Flanagan
* Terence Brady	Ann Atkinson	Thomas Flanagan
* Peter Brady	James Smith	Hugh Flanagan
* Philip Brady	Sally Pagin	Philip Chapman
Philip Traner	Simon Daly	Peter Everet
Francis Traner	Catherine Daly	William Murtagh
* John Traner	Patrick McRooney	+ Charles Armstrong
Catherine Traner	Bernard McJooney	Bernard Clark
Mary Traner	James Healy	Anthony O'Reilly
Rose Traner	Terence O'Neil	Nicholas Bean
William McCaffery	Felix O'Neil	* Children.
James McCaffery	James Wall	+ U.S. Citizen.

126

Advertisements

John M'Cracken, lately from Belfast, advertises his trade in turned
wood, bobbins, iron and brass ware, thread mills, weavers' instruments,
etc.

Seeking R. K. Dowling, a native of Queen's County, Ireland, lately
residing in New York.

January 4, 1812

Seeking John James and Ross M'Guire, who emigrated from Cole Island,
County Tyrone, about 16 years ago. Enquiry made by Ross M'Guire, son of
John, who recently arrived.

July 25, 1812

Seeking John Morrin, carpenter, son of George Morrin of Londonderry,
who arrived in Philadelphia in 1808 aboard the Ship Eliza, Captain
Church; he resided lately in Baltimore. His sister Sarah resided near
Philadelphia.

August 29, 1812

Seeking Robert Seaton, formerly of Balliboley, north Ireland, who
migrated to Pennsylvania around 1792.

Seeking John Grier, native of Roghan, Derrynoose parish, County Armagh,
who sailed from Londonderry aboard the John Atkinson, July, 1811, bound
for Philadelphia. His brother Joseph lives in Kingston Falls, Ulster
County, New York.

January 9, 1813

Died December 30, John Smilie, native of County Down, aged 74 years,
migrated to America in 1762 and settled in Lancaster, Pa. (long obituary)

January 30, 1813

Seeking Joseph Farrell, son of John Farrell of Leadentown, near
Middletown, Co. Cork. Sailed from England to New York and not heard from
since. By Laurence Farrell & Sons, Blacksmiths, Boston.

Seeking Thomas Patterson, from the parish of Loch Patrick, County
Tyrone; about five years ago he was teaching school in Middle Island,
Bartley County, Virginia, but he crossed the Allegany Mountains and has
not been heard from since. By his brother Samuel Patterson.

February 6, 1813

" Mrs. Bell Kennedy, who was carried into the Island of St. ,John's,
or Halifax, by the British, on her passage from Londonderry (Ireland)
to the U. States, is hereby informed that her husband, Henry Kennedy, is

now in the city of New York, at the house of Mr. James Hunter No 6
James Slip, where he shall be happy to hear from her and his six children
who were taken with her."

Seeking John and Mary Coleman, who sailed from Dublin at the end of
June or first part of July last for this country. By Mr. John Kenny,
merchant, of Charleston, S.C.

"If Wm. M'Garrigle who sailed from Baltimore for France in the
Schooner Arrow, in December, 1811, has returned to the United States,
he is hereby informed that his Father and Family now reside in New York,
corner of Water St. and Beckman Slip, and will be happy to hear from him."

April 10, 1813

Died in Philadelphia, April 3, Peter Farley, a native of County Cavan,
aged 32 years.

June 5, 1813

Last Thursday was buried at St. Patrick's, Patrick Byrne, age 24,
a volunteer in the 3d Regiment, who was shot at Fort Columbus on May 29
for mutiny. He had migrated about 14 years ago at his uncle's request.

Seeking Joseph Stewart, a native of Clogher, Co. Tyrone, who migrated
before the American Revolution and settled (it is believed) in the
Carolinas. By Peter Smith, Prof. of Music, New York.

July 9, 1814

"---- Reed, a native of the county of Antrim (Ireland) was shot
yesterday at Fort Columbus, for desertion, pursuant to athe sentence of
a court-martial."

November 5, 1814

Died on November 2, Mrs. Margaret Harin, aged 38 years, wife of Mr.
Patrick Harin, residing at No. 47 Duane Street in New York, formerly of
the county of Sligo, Ireland. Burial at St. Patrick's.

December 10, 1814

Seeking Patrick Scanlon, a native of Ireland, who came to the United
States about 12 years ago and was married in Franklin County, North
Carolina, about six years ago, which place he left about three years ago
for New Orleans.

November 4, 1815

Died at Pittsburg, Rev. Thomas M'Grain, aged 40 years, a native of
the city of Dublin.

January 27, 1816

Died in New York city on Tuesday, of a lingering illness, Mr. William Tennant, a native of Belfast, Ireland.

February 3, 1816

Died suddenly on Sunday last, at Monroe-works, Orange County, New York, Patrick Kelley, aged about 35 years, a native of Upper-Ormond, Queens County, Ireland.

March 9, 1816

Died in New York city on February 28, aged 32, Mr. Anthony Callaghan, a native of the parish of Clune, county of Leitrim, Ireland, whence he removed to this city in the year 1801.

March 23, 1816

Died in Spartansburg, S.C. on the 29th January, Mrs. Sarah Penny, aged 103 years, 7 months and 14 days. This venerable and much esteemed Lady was a native of the county of Down, Ireland.

April 6, 1816

Died in New York City on Marcy 28, aged 65, Mrs. Margaret Godfrey, a native of the parish of Sallahud, county of Tipperary, Ireland.

April 13, 1816

Died in New York City, Patrick M'Kenna, aged 40 years, a native of the parish of Fahan, county of Donegal, Ireland.

April 20, 1816

Died in New York City on Monday last, of a lingering illness, in the 31st year of his age, Mr. Gerald M'Enery, a native of Killarney in the county of Kerry, Ireland.

Died on December 8, in the 99th year of his age, David Maconaughy, Esq., of Menallen township, Adams Co, Pa. He came from Ireland to this country about the 21st year of his age.

April 27, 1816

Died in New York City, John Reilly, aged 28 years, a native of King's Court, county of Cavan, Ireland.

May 18, 1816

Died on Manday at Brooklyn, Mrs. Jane Wilson, aged 72, a native of Armagh, Ireland.

Died on the 3d inst., at Baltimore, Mr. Bernard Dougherty, aged 38 years, a native of Carn, county of Donegal, Ireland.

July 6, 1816

Died yesterday in New York City, Mr. Edward Connolly, a native of Co. Monaghan, Ireland.

July 20, 1816

Died at York, Pennsylvania on the 30th of May, Hugh M'Aleer, aged 23 years, a native of Dromore, County Tyrone.

Died at York on the 13th of June, Michael M'Aleer, aged 28 years, a native of Dromore, County Tyrone.

Died at York on the 28th of May, Farrel Ternam, a native of the county of Leitrim.

Died at York on the 7th of June, Peter Murphy, a native of the county of Antrim.

August 3, 1816

Seeking Nessrs. Jerome O'Calloghan and Patrick O'Callaghan, who arrived in the United States from Co. Cork about 18 or 19 years ago; lived for a time at Albany and then in Aurelius in Cayuga County.

December 14, 1816

Died in New York City, on the 27th of November, aged 23 years, Mr. Richard W. Usher, a native of Birr in King's County, Ireland.

January 25, 1817

Died at New London, Conn., on the 20th inst., Mr. John Driscoll, aged 60 years, a native of Cloyne, Co. Cork. (Had taken part in the rebellion of 1798)

February 8, 1817

Seeking James Cussack who sailed from Ireland for the United States in April last.

May 31, 1817

Seeking John Keating, who came from Cork to New York in the ship Margaret.

June 28, 1817

Died at Nashville, Tenn., on the 5th of June, Mr. James Hanna, in the 47th year of his age. He was a native of Banbridge, Co. Down. He is survived by his widow, a daughter of Mr. James Jackson of Ballibay, Co. Monaghan.

July 5, 1817

Died at Baltimore on June 30, Mr. Henry Jackson, formerly of Dublin.

Index to Names of Vessels

Index to Names of Captains

Passenger
Surname Index

Abbott 15-11;16-1
Abercromby 16-11
Acheson 16-9
Adair 16-19,31
Adams 11-25,51;12-18,32;16-32
Aeggs 16-42
Agnew 15-9
Aigue 12-29
Aidwell 16-6
Aiken 11-3,14;12-9;16-50
Aikens 11-15
Akin 11-15
Alchorn 11-18
Alcorn 11-38;12-10
Alexander 11-16;12-10;15-16;16-25,
            31,46
Alges 11-44
Allen 12-7,19;15-21;16-2,11,21,40,49;
        17-3
Alligan 12-2
Alsop 11-2
Amact 16-19
Amberson 11-6
Anderlay 12-6
Anderson 11-1,8,9,25,38,51;12-1,17;
            15-9,23;16-9,16,28,32,45,50
Andre 16-2
Andrews 11-4,18;15-24;16-3
Androhan 11-54
Anna 12-15
Anthony 11-25
Ardis 16-1
Arenner 11-44
Armitage 11-20
Armstrong 11-6,14,21,35,56;12-5,18;
            15-8,16,18;16-12,29,31,48;
            17-15,29
Arnold 15-2;16-2,18;17-7
Arthur 11-38;16-50;17-23
Ash 16-8
Ashworth 12-4
Aslein 11-1
Asley 16-2
Asple 16-3
Atcheson 11-44;16-40
Atkins 11-16
Atkinson 11-42;13-1;15-18;16-3;17-29
Auchanan 16-12
Auld 11-1,56
Austin 16-19
Auston 12-13
Aunis 16-37
Avery 17-27

Babe 17-26
Bacon 11-43;16-18
Bailey 11-38;12-15;17-15,17
Bailie 16-30,33;17-2,21
Baimbrick 11-24
Baird 16-22,25,28
Bakey 12-3
Baland 16-34
Baldwin 12-3
Ball 15-18
Ballagh 16-8
Ballentine 16-45
Bambrick 11-24;16-20
Ban 17-1
Banecan 11-4
Banin 16-7
Bankhead 16-32
Banks 16-28
Bannan 15-2
Banner 11-31
Barbadge 16-2
Barbonr 16-33
Barclay 17-22,29
Bare 16-6
Barker 16-42
Barklie 11-56
Barlow 12-14
Barnes 12-5,27
Barnett 11-46;15-18
Barney 11-16
Barns 11-25
Barr 11-40;12-19;16-28,45
Barron 11-42
Barrow 15-21
Barry 10-1;11-5;15-2;16-6
Barton 12-8;17-2,3,21
Basey 12-3
Bayley 16-28
Baxter 16-45
Beadle 17-4
Beahan 17-8
Bean 17-29
Beattie 16-33
Beatty 11-6,18,44,53,60;12-19;16-13,42
Beaty 12-17,19;17-1
Beck 12-13;17-1
Bedlow 12-12
Bednard 16-28
Beerman 16-37
Beggs 15-18
Begley 11-60;12-19
Behan 15-2
Beil 12-19

135

Bell 11-1,4,16,58;12-5,14;15-8,18;
     16-8,30,42,50;17-14
Bennet 11-62
Bennett 11-18,40;16-37
Benningham 16-53
Benton 16-2
Bergin 16-48
Bernard 16-35
Berney 16-5
Berry 16-35;17-9
Best 11-8,26;12-39
Beverly 16-32
Bill 12-14
Binne 16-5
Binns 17-8
Bird 11-24
Birk 11-24;15-10
Birns 11-25
Birwin 12-10
Bishop 10-1
Black 11-55,58;12-5,17,27;15-18;16-10,
     24,51;17-2
Blackely 17-17
Blair 11-42,51,56;12-10;15-16;16-22,30,
     45
Blake 11-5
Blakely 15-9
Blame 15-9
Blanchfield 15-4
Blaney 12-10
Blany 11-14
Bleakley 15-9
Bleakly 10-1;12-27
Blean 17-24
Blood 15-6
Bloomer 12-14
Bloomfield 12-19;16-18
Blythe 11-21;17-15
Boak 12-28
Bodd 11-14
Boden 15-8;17-22
Bodkins 12-7
Boggs 11-55;16-25
Bogle 15-16
Bohan 16-4
Boke 16-50
Bolton 16-18
Bonar 11-53
Bond 16-50
Bonnel 11-6
Bonner 11-10;12-7
Boogs 12-30
Booney 11-42
Booth 17-2,21,23
Borlridge 16-21

Borr 16-19
Borskin 16-28
Bossman 12-31
Botham 16-50
Bowen 11-40
Bowles 10-1
Boyce 16-48
Boyd 11-8,15,42,44,51;12-15,27;16-6
     12,23,30,32,42;17-17
Boyle 11-16,25,26,44;12-19,32;15-10
     16;16-9,14,29;17-17,20,21
Bradely 12-29
Bradford 12-5;16-42
Bradley 11-19,59;12-33;16-14,21,28,
     29,37,42;17-15
Brady 11-9;12-7;15-2,3,6,10;16-2,3,
     35,47;17-9,14,24,28,29
Brainerd 16-49
Braith 15-5
Branely 16-49
Branick 16-48
Branigon 11-20
Brankin 16-11
Brannon 12-1
Bratton 12-40
Brawley 16-50
Braydon 17-28
Bream 16-7
Breen 12-19,27
Breman 16-48
Bremar 11-60
Brennan 12-39;16-28,34,48;17-10
Bresland 12-19
Brett 17-7
Briarty 11-60
Bride 16-34
Bridge 11-42
Bridges 16-2
Bridget 11-14
Brien 12-8
Briggs 16-53
Britton 15-16
Brogan 11-25;15-19
Bronnigan ? 12-5
Brooks 12-14;15-16
Brophy 16-5,21
Bropigan 15-20
Brown 11-1,2,4,7,18,21,55,58;12-1,5,
     11,14,19,27,33;15-9,10,16,17,
     23;16-12,17,26,28,29,39,48;17-
     7,23,24
Browne 11-51;16-14
Bruce 13-1
Bryan 11-44;12-4
Bryd 16-32

Bryson 11-40
Buchan 16-51
Buchanan 11-35;15-16
Buchannon 11-14
Buckley 11-5
Budden 16-17
Buden 11-59
Buher 16-30
Bull 11-5,51
Bullen 11-5
Bunham 11-4
Burchill 16-27
Burk 11-14;16-28,49
Burke 11-43;16-4,14,37,47;17-21
Burlugh 17-14
Burn 16-5;17-14
Burnes 11-16
Burns 11-6,9,16,58;12-11,12,18;15-16,
    19;16-22,33;17-14
Burnside 16-32
Burr 16-24
Burrows 17-24
Burt 12-30
Burton 11-24
Butler 10-1;16-28
Butterley 16-37
Butterworth 15-12
Buttle 16-35
Byers 16-31,32
Byres 12-10
Byrne 11-19;12-15,34;15-2,17;16-2,4,
    6,18,20;17-11,27;6/5/13
Byrnes 10-1;16-18;17-22
Byrue 17-11
Caberty 17-21
Caffer 17-18
Cafferty 16-28
Caffrey 11-19
Caffry 15-2
Caher 17-18
Cain 16-28
Caires 12-5
Cairns 16-40
Caldwell 11-16,59;12-6,13,17,28,39;
    15-23;16-6;17-1,21
Calgan 16-22
Calhoun 15-23;16-28
Callaghan 11-29;15-3;16-2,28,38,39;
    17-11;3/9/16
Callahand 11-62
Callihan 11-5
Callon 17-29
Calloway 12-4
Calney 16-8
Calshan 16-2

Calvin 11-14
Cam 16-39
Cambell 11-42
Camble 11-6,8;16-50
Cameron 17-22
Cammins 11-60
Campbell 11-1,7,18,35,42,58,59;
    12-17,33;13-1;15-5,9,10;
    16-1,22,26,30,32,33,39,40,
    42,51;17-11
Cancannon 11-20
Canghey 16-10
Canigan 16-22
Cannelan 16-33
Cannon 11-9,15,16,43;15-16;16-47
Cannoughton 16-47
Canway 16-33
Carabine 16-50
Caralsey 12-5
Carden 11-20
Carey 11-5;12-32;16-26
Carlan 16-50
Carland 12-10
Carle 16-5
Carlin 15-9;16-28
Carling 11-16
Carlisle 12-7;15-18
Carlton 11-6;16-30
Carmachy 16-50
Carmeran 16-50
Carmichael 15-5
Carn 12-2
Carney 12-3,32;16-5,24,28;17-21
Carolan 11-38;17-8
Carr 11-2,26,44;12-5;15-23;16-22,32,
    40,53
Carrall 11-19,40
Carrigan 11-7;12-30;16-24;17-15
Carrol 12-2
Carroll 15-2;16-34,45;17-28
Carse 11-4
Carslile 16-23
Carson 11-15;12-11;16-1,29
Cartan 11-55
Carter 15-16
Cartwright 17-11
Caruthers 16-30
Caselly 16-53
Casey 11-5,58;12-10;15-21;17-10,19
Casher 16-36
Cassady 15-3;16-8
Cassell 16-51
Cassely 11-26
Cassidy 11-8,25,60;12-17,27,30;17-27
Castello 16-33,49

137

140

Fife 11-18;16-40
Finegan 15-6
Fingusin 15-5
Finigan 16-12,19,37;17-18
Finlan 11-60;16-33
Finlay 11-14;16-28;17-13
Finn 12-2,19;16-17
Finnegan 11-25
Finney 11-20
Finnigan 17-28
Finniston 12-40
Fioheley 16-49
Fisher 16-22,32
Fitch 17-14
Fitzgerald 10-1;11-19;15-10,18,19
Fitzpatrick 11-19;16-3,5,35
Fitzsimmons 11-26;12-14
Fitzsimons 11-26
Flaherty 15-16;16-17
Flanagan 11-18;16-4,18,33,47;17-29
Flanery 11-20
Flanigan 11-58
Fleming 12-34
Flemming 11-21;12-10;16-35
Fletcher 11-16,60;12-1,19
Flinn 16-9,21
Flood 15-4,5
Floughsby 10-1
Floyd 11-25;12-13
Flurn 16-7
Flushing 16-37
Flyn 11-55;16-6
Foaley 11-5
Fodraham 12-8
Fogerty 11-5
Foley 11-24;16-33,34
Folin 16-49
Folly 11-24
Forbes 16-50
Forcade 11-14
Forest 16-6
Forley 11-20
Forsyth 11-4;15-9,16
Fortune 16-14;17-28
Foster 11-15;15-9;12-29;15-12
Fothall 11-18
Fowey 11-5
Fox 15-19
Frame 15-16
Frances 11-1
Francis 16-1;17-15
Frasier 11-9
Frayne 15-17
Frazer 15-8
Freal 16-33

Freeborn 11-7;12-10
Freeland 11-56
Freeman 11-5;17-8
Froster 11-55
Fullam 11-31
Fullan 11-14
Fuller 11-58
Fullerton 12-1
Fulton 11-14,25;12-31;16-22
Fuman 16-49
Funston 11-7;15-16
Furlong 10-1;12-3;16-20,36;17-28
Gaffin 11-56
Gafney 15-6;17-14
Galbraith 11-53;12-10,11;15-16,1ᵉ
Galbreath 15-19
Galey 16-26,34
Gallager 16-29
Gallagher 11-60;12-13,31;15-16,2ᵉ
          16-13,25,33;17-15,27
Gallaher 12-7,8,17,19
Gallaugher 11-51;12-40
Gallbraith 16-28
Gallen 11-51
Gallery 11-8
Galliher 12-10
Gallivan 11-5
Galsngher 16-51
Gamble 11-4,8;16-22
Gamel 15-3
Ganly 16-7
Ganner 16-47
Gannon 16-47
Ganway 16-50
Garagan 12-8
Gardner 15-8;16-32;17-4,13
Garelan 16-7
Garnett 17-10
Garney 16-18
Garrett 15-8
Garry 12-8
Garven 16-28
Garvin 11-2
Gatt 11-14,25
Gault 15-16,23;16-29
Gausley 16-31
Geary 16-6
Geery 17-2
Gelison 11-6
Gelston 11-8
Genagul 11-18
Gent 17-7
Geoffrey 17-7
Geoghegan 15-10
Geohegan 16-41

143

Hair 16-31
Hale 15-24
Hales 10-1
Hall 11-1,6,15,21,44;16-29;17-9
Halle 16-37
Halligan 17-28
Hallugan 11-19
Halpen 16-36
Halpin 16-9
Hamard 11-7
Hamill 11-7,51
Hamilton 11-4,6,7,8,18,42,51;12-7,11,
     28,29,30,32,33;16-26,30,31;
     17-8,9,21
Hammill 16-12
Hammond 16-28,29
Hanagan 11-7
Handerson 15-20
Handfield 16-46
Handlen 17-28
Hanff 16-14
Hanlan 11-7,51
Hanley 12-27;16-37;17-8
Hanlon 16-2
Hanly 17-8
Hanna 16-19;6/28/17
Hannagan 17-15
Hannah 11-5,43
Hannsberry 17-28
Hansbrow 12-34
Hanshaw 11-15Hapan 12-19
Hapan 12-19
Haran 16-49
Harbison 15-8;16-26
Harcourt 12-5;15-23
Hardgraves 17-18
Harding 11-24,29;16-35
Hardman 16-47
Hardy 16-45
Hargaden 16-33
Hargon 16-50
Harin 11/5/14
Harkin 11-15;12-32;16-28,33,48
Harman 11-20
Harold 12-30
Harper 11-21;12-7;16-11,12
Harpur 11-58;16-20
Harrington 17-16
Harris 11-21,42;12-17;15-9
Harrison 11-1,8,60;16-18;17-14
Harrold 11-54
Harshaw 11-8,25
Hart 15-12;16-33,34,52
Hartley 11-21

Hartness 16-50
Harver 11-15
Harvey 11-1,18;12-6,8;16-8,28
Hasdy 12-6
Haskett 11-5
Haslam 11-25
Haslett 15-18
Hassan 16-50
Hassen 16-50
Hasting 11-55
Hatch 12-34;16-20
Haughey 11-16   Haviland 17
Hawkins 16-22
Hawthorn 11-14,58;16-20,35
Hay 12-1;16-8,29,31,49
Hayden 15-4;16-14
Hayes 17-19
Hays 16-40
Hayson 11-21
Hazelton 11-16
Hazleton 11-14,53;12-18
Healy 11-60;16-2,33,49;17-13,29
Heany 16-35
Hearn 10-1
Hector 11-38
Heekey 12-3
Heely 16-16
Henderson 11-9,25,44,60;12-13,32;1
     16,17;16-12,27,30,49,50
     17-17,20
Hendrea 12-10
Hendrick 16-6
Henegan 16-34
Henney 15-6
Henphill 11-55
Henry 11-4,16,21,26,55;12-7,15,17,
     27,28,32;15-8;16-8,41,49,52;
     17-24
Heran 11-14
Herker 11-14
Herran 16-23
Herrin 15-5
Herron 12-33
Heson 11-14
Hetherington 16-32
Hewett 15-2
Hewit 16-13
Hiate 12-5
Hice 15-8
Hickings 11-16
Hicks 12-17;16-17
Hickson 17-19
Higgins 16-15,34
Hill 15-8;16-18,19,28,32,33,49

145

Keirnan 16-35
Keith 12-15;16-8
Kelley 11-55,59;12-1,29;2/3/16
Kelly 10-1;11-14,15,19,40,55;12-7,8,
    19,30,33,39;15-2,12,17;16-4,7,
    14,19,23,28,33,36,37,41,48;
    17-3,14,16,20,21,28
Kemple 15-6
Kench 11-62
Kenedy 16-48
Kenmaer 11-3
Kennady 16-21
Kennedy 11-1,6,9,43,46;12-14,32;15-10,
    19;16-5,28,31,33,37,42;17-8,10,
    13,17,22,23,28;2/6/13
Kenney 11-20
Kenny 11-20;12-8;13-1;16-5;17-7;2/6/13
Kent 11-5
Keogh 12-4
Keon 12-6
Keown 15-10
Ker 11-9,53
Kerby 16-6
Kernaghan 15-16
Kernan 17-18
Kernard 12-10
Kerr 11-7,16,31,38,51,60;12-1,11,19,
    28,30;15-3,16;16-10,25
Kervan 16-41
Kerwan 11-19;16-47
Kettell 12-6
Key 11-18
Keys 16-26;17-1
Kidd 16-18
Kiegan 17-11
Kield 16-1
Kilfeather 12-2
Kilfoyle 16-47
Kilgallen 11-60
Kilgent 12-7
Kilkenny 17-13
Killbride 11-60
Killen 15-6;17-10,17
Killihan 12-8
Killy 11-15
Kilmartin 16-33,49
Kinanak 16-37
Kinch 11-20
King 11-24;12-10,30;15-12;16-11;17-21
Kingsland 16-40
Kingston 12-13
Kinkede 12-31
Kinsela 12-3
Kinshela 16-20
Kirk 11-35,55,58;12-7;15-23

Kirkby 11-5;17-16
Kirkpatrick 11-7,51;12-18;15-23;
    16-8,26,28
Kirkwood 12-40
Kirr 11-16
Kittrick 12-4
Knaggs 17-11
Knox 11-2,42,44,51;12-39;15-16
Kumely 12-4
Kyle 12-40;15-16;16-45;17-20
Kynn 16-6
Lacey 11-24
Lacy 11-24
Laffey 16-15
Lagee 12-32
Lain 16-14
Laird 12-30;15-16
Lally 16-47
Lalor 16-39
Lamb 11-6
Lambert 11-7;15-17;16-47,53
Lammin 12-34
Lane 11-5;16-48
Langer 11-24
Langley 15-17
Langton 16-20
Lanigan 11-20
Lankey 17-26
Laperty 16-28
Laphen 16-53
Laplin 11-19
Lappin 12-15
Lapsy 11-56
Largey 16-46
Larkie 11-18
Larkin 10-1;12-1;16-39;17-21
Larn 12-32
Lathem 15-8,12;16-39
Laughery 16-28
Laughlin 12-5,28;16-28,31
Laughran 16-31
Laughton 16-46
Laverty 11-18,42
Law 11-1,31;12-18;16-13,32;
    17-14,22
Lawler 11-20;16-41
Lawn 16-28
Lawson 12-28
Lea 15-10
Leady 12-4
Leahy 16-39
Leaky 11-5
Lear 12-13;15-1
Leary 11-19;16-34
Leckey 12-14

Lecky 16-28
Leddy 16-3,35
Lee 15-8,9;17-10
Leech 11-43;16-50,51
Leggit 17-1
Leman 11-56
Lemen 12-28
Lennox 12-2
Lenon 11-7
Lenox 17-17
Leonard 10-1;12-17,27,29
Lester 15-23
Lett 16-17
Leviston 11-21
Lewis 11-5;12-15
Leyden 11-60
Lietson 11-1
Ligget 12-27
Lightell 12-13
Lighton 16-50
Lilly 16-47
Limerick 16-22
Linchey 16-45
Lindsay 11-15,44;15-3;16-34,42;17-20,24
Lingan 16-34
Linn 15-5
Linnan 16-53
Linnen 11-5
Lipsett 12-8
Liston 11-1
Lithgow 12-32
Little 11-9,15;16-33;17-24
Lockat 11-14
Lockery 11-21
Lockhart 12-39;15-16
Lockwood 16-48
Logan 11-7,9,14,51;12-10,11;15-16;16-9
Logg 12-8
Loghland 12-10
Logue 11-51
Long 11-29,44;12-5,19;16-6,48
Longman 15-9
Loony 15-23
Louergan 12-3
Loughern 12-1
Lougherty 12-11
Loughery 12-28
Loughead 11-51;12-30
Loughlin 11-60
Loughman 16-5
Loughry 12-10
Love 11-55;15-16;16-28
Low 15-9
Lowden 15-16
Lowery 17-20

Lowry 11-6;16-46;17-22
Lucas 16-37
Lucky 12-14
Lucus 11-20
Luke 11-42;16-1
Lurkie 11-18
Lynch 11-54;12-10;15-2,19,21;16-28,52
Lyndon 16-17
Lynes 16-14
Lynn 11-21;12-11
Lyon 12-8
Lyons 11-7,16,25;16-19;17-17
M'Afee 12-18
M'Affer 16-40
M'Aleer 7/20/16
M'Alester 12-33
M'Alister 16-8,50
M'Allignon 16-32
M'Allisted 11-9
M'Allister 11-21
M'Aloo 16-28
M'Alpin 11-8
M'Alvin 11-55
M'Analty 16-52
M'Anary 12-27
M'Andrew 11-60
M'Anorney 11-14
M'Anulty 11-15
M'Arand 16-16
M'Arann 12-30
M'Ardle 16-18
M'Arnon 15-6
M'Arthur 11-38
M'Aspin 11-44
M'Atier 15-8
M'Atter 11-8
M'Auley 16-5
M'Avenny 12-27
M'Bea 12-13
M'Braty 16-24
M'Bride 11-40,60;12-13,29,31;15-5;
          16-23,26,28,42;17-22,24
M'Brien 10-1
M'Brier 12-5
M'Brine 11-18
M'Burney 11-26
M'Cabe 10-1;15-2;16-10,35;17-26
M'Cafferty 11-7,51;12-8
M'Caffery 12-27;17-29
M'Caffrey 17-27
M'Caffry 12-17
M'Caird 11-14
M'Calden 12-28
M'Caliman 17-23
M'Call 16-11

M'Callan 16-50
M'Calluch 12-33
M'Cally 17-20
M'Cam 16-23
M'Cambridge 15-9;16-32;17-22
M'Cammar 11-14
M'Can 12-32
M'Canaghty 16-40
M'Conaghy 16-50
M'Canbrey 16-13
M'Cance 11-1
M'Cane 11-9
M'Canly 16-13
M'Cann 12-5;15-5,10;16-18,25;17-27
M'Canna 17-22
M'Cannell 16-20
M'Carden 15-5
M'Carfin 16-2
M'Carker 16-40
M'Carter 12-13;15-13
M'Carthy 16-48
M'Cartin 12-3;17-17
M'Cartney 11-4,14;16-42;17-2,24
M'Carton 11-8
M'Carty 15-5
M'Caskey 12-27,29;16-9
M'Casle 15-10
M'Caughall 11-7
M'Caughan 11-25
M'Cauley 16-26
M'Cauly 16-9,16,42
M'Causland 16-32
M'Cave 17-21
M'Cawl 17-6
M'Cawley 11-4;16-31
M'Cay 16-22
M'Clane 11-19
M'Claskey 12-10;16-28,29
M'Clatchey 12-15
M'Clay 12-31
M'Clean 11-56;16-30
M'Cleary 15-5
M'Cleery 12-30
M'Cleland 12-5
M'Clelland 12-40;15-9;17-23
M'Clellon 15-9
M'Clenaghan 11-26
M'Cleyen 12-3
M'Clory 17-24
M'Closkey 11-38;12-1
M'Closky 12-29
M'Cloud 16-51
M'Cloy 11-21
M'Clure 11-42,59;12-8
M'Clushey 16-23

M'Coal 16-22
M'Colgan 12-18,32;16-26,28
M'Colgin 11-44
M'Colim 15-16
M'Colley 11-16;12-13;16-18
M'Collison 15-16
M'Collough 16-31
M'Collum 12-19;16-13
M'Comally 12-17
M'Comb 11-4,21;12-8,14;16-50
M'Conaghy 11-21
M'Conaway 12-1
M'Conlay 11-16
M'Conley 16-40
M'Connaghy 11-21
M'Connell 11-6,21,38,58;16-48;17-2
M'Conway 11-16
M'Cool 16-50
M'Cormack 15-3
M'Cormick 11-20;12-11,19,31;16-31,
48;17-13
M'Cormik 16-15
M'Cosker 11-55
M'Coskery 11-8
M'Cousland 11-25
M'Cown 11-51
M'Coy 11-55;12-28
M'Cracken 11-4;16-1;9/21/11
M'Crane 12-27
M'Crea 12-28;16-29;17-9
M'Cready 11-7,55;12-30
M'Creely 11-31
M'Creery 11-25
M'Croghan 12-1
M'Crossin 16-51
M'Cue 11-25,51
M'Cullagh 15-1
M'Cullough 11-6,56;17-9,21,22
M'Cully 11-4;12-10
M'Cune 11-26
M'Curdy 11-1,18;15-9,18
M'Curry 11-6
M'Curtney 11-14
M'Cusker 16-50
M'Custer 12-17
M'Cuthen 16-5
M'Daid 12-28,30;16-22
M'Dangal 16-51
M'Dangall 16-51
M'Daniel 15-6;16-2,42,48
M'Dead 12-32
M'Demiott 16-21
M'Dermot 11-55;12-34;16-48
M'Dermott 12-2;16-4,20,22,27,41;17-
M'Devill 11-59

148

149

M'Ilereavy 12-18
M'Ilhames 16-29
M'Ilheny 16-51
M'Illoy 12-17
M'Ilrath 15-9
M'Ilroy 11-25;16-1,42
M'Ilwain 12-19
M'Indov 11-58
M'Intire 11-18,60;12-8,19;15-16;16-42
M'Intosh 16-51
M'Intyre 12-1
M'Irish 17-23
M'Kagh 11-55
M'Kardy 11-5
M'Kay 11-51;15-5,10;16-20,30;17-22
M'Kean 16-45;17-6
M'Kee 11-4,8,55;12-10,30;15-5;16-18,19;
    17-2
M'Keene 16-30
M'Keever 12-8;17-15
M'Keighan 16-32
M'Kelery 11-8
M'Kell 16-1
M'Kenna 17-18;4/13/16
M'Kennen 12-33
M'Kenney 11-58
M'Kennon 15-18
M'Kenny 11-4
M'Kenzie 11-1
M'Keon 12-5,7
M'Keoun 17-21
M'Keown 16-50
M'Kernan 15-12
M'Kever 11-56
M'Kevers 16-14
M'Key 11-5,8,19,58;16-16
M'Kibbin 12-15
M'Kie 11-21
M'Kill 16-40
M'Kim 12-19
M'Kindry 12-18
M'Kinlay 11-7
M'Kinley 11-38;12-8;13-1;17-20
M'Kinne 16-32
M'Kinney 11-59;17-21
M'Kinstry 16-12
M'Knight 11-18
M'Kninon 16-33
M'Knott 11-44
M'Korkell 12-13
M'Kosker 11-15
M'Lachling 15-23
M'Lain 16-39
M'Lance 11-1
M'Lanna 11-1

M'Lary 11-7
M'Laughlin 11-7,38,51;12-13,17,18,
    29,30,32;16-18,22,25,28
    33,40,45,47,50,51,53
M'Lawry 16-46
M'Lean 12-30,34;15-3,9;16-3
M'Leer 12-17
M'Lentock 17-7
M'Leon 11-18
M'Linchy 16-45
M'Loghlin 12-10
M'Lorlan 11-15
M'Lorran 16-40
M'Lorten 11-18
M'Lory 12-15
M'Loughlin 16-28;17-26
M'Magan 11-8
M'Magun 11-8
M'Mahan 11-6
M'Mahin 11-35
M'Mahon 11-9;15-19;17-10
M'Mail 16-40
M'Malin 11-59
M'Mally 10-1
M'Manimin 12-10
M'Manns 16-3,49
M'Mannyman 11-16
M'Manus 11-43,59;12-8,17;15-2,3;
    16-19,35
M'Marrow 16-49
M'Master 12-1
M'Meehan 11-8
M'Menamy 11-7;16-22
M'Mennamy 11-7
M'Mennomy 11-55
M'Menomy 16-28,50,51
M'Millan 17-22
M'Miller 15-16
M'Minimin 11-55
M'Muldoon 12-27
M'Mullan 11-3,4;12-7,17
M'Mullen 11-46,58;12-10,13;15-5;
    16-8;17-17
M'Murdy 12-7
M'Murray 11-1,31,62;16-8
M'Murrey 11-3
M'Murry 16-40
M'Nally 12-15;17-29
M'Nama 16-50
M'Namara 12-28
M'Narney 16-2
M'Natuig 12-32
M'Naughton 15-9
M'Naugton 16-17
M'Neal 11-25,51

150

M'Neil 12-28	Mackeon 15-18
M'Neill 11-31,46	Mackerill 16-40
M'Neilly 11-56	Mackeson 16-3
M'Nenagh 17-18	Mackey 12-4,5,15,32
M'Neremon 15-16	Maconaughy 4/20/16
M'Nought 11-25	Macy 13-1
M'Nulty 12-13,17;16-33	Madden 11-7,46;12-3;15-12;16-2
M'Paul 12-17	Madigan 15-19
M'Peak 11-2	Maffett 11-21
M'Pharland 11-44	Magee 12-15,40;16-1,11,14,42;17-24
M'Philaney 16-50	Magell 11-4
M'Philown 16-49	Magher 16-32
M'Poland 17-26	Magill 15-23;16-1;17-17
M'Quade 11-58	Maginnis 12-2
M'Queen 16-40	Magis 11-18
M'Quid 12-13	Magrah 17-10
M'Quide 12-17	Maguinis 11-6
M'Quig 16-42	Maguire 15-15;17-10
M'Quillin 11-17	Mahaffy 11-26
M'Quinn 16-18	Mahany 16-30
M'Quoid 15-18;17-22	Maher 12-4;17-1
M'Ralin 15-9	Mahers 17-28
M'Redden 16-32	Mahon 16-17,35
M'Ree 17-24	Mahony 15-4;16-6
M'Rooney 17-29	Maiben 15-17
M'Rride 17-22	Maitland 11-59
M'Serley 16-50	Malcomson 11-31;16-13
M'Shae 12-8	Malone 15-2,6
M'Shane 11-51;15-16;17-4	Maloney 11-5
M'Shee 12-8	Malowney 11-5
M'Sheldon 15-10	Malsey 16-25
M'Sherry 16-33	Malvin 10-1
M'Swigan 16-50	Maly 16-5
M'Taggart 12-8	Manely 11-16
M'Tahan 16-42	Maney 11-14
M'Tea 16-23	Manly 10-1
M'Ternan 17-13	Manning 16-23
M'Thilfry 12-10	Mansfield 11-15
M'Tice 16-42	Mansger 12-4
M'Tier 11-8;17-26	Manson 11-51
M'Togert 11-38	Mape 17-16
M'Turner 12-31	Mara 16-52
M'Vaid 16-50	March 15-10
M'Vea 11-8;12-33;16-31	Marfelt 16-4
M'Veagh 11-55	Mark 11-6
M'Veigh 16-50	Markey 16-8
M'Vey 11-21	Marks 11-17
M'Vicker 15-18	Marmian 17-21
M'Voy 16-28	Maron 11-4
M'Waters 12-27	Marrow 16-11
M'Whatey 11-4	Marshal 12-33
M'Wherter 11-4	Marshall 11-7;15-9;16-42;17-23
M'Williams 12-33	Martagh 17-10
M'----thine 12-17	

Martin 11-3,14,21,38,42,43,52,55,60;
    12-2,8,17,18;15-3,9;16-2,9,13,
    24,26,32,35,40,42,45;17-15,24
Mason 12-6,14;15-3;16-41
Masterson 11-55;15-2;16-35
Materson 17-7
Mathew 11-44
Mathews 11-24,56;12-29;15-8;16-48;
    17-10,25
Mathewson 11-15;16-51
Matterson 17-7
Maurice 16-42
Maxwell 11-9;15-9,16;16-12,53
Mayberry 12-30
Maze 11-18
Mead 16-5
Meader 12-4
Mearse 17-27
Mecham 17-13
Mechan 11-15;12-6;15-16;16-28
Mechlan 16-33
Medile 15-24
Meeghan 11-20
Meehan 11-60
Mehain 12-19
Meharg 11-6
Mein 16-33
Meloy 16-31
Memna 12-31
Menteur 11-24
Mention 11-8
Metchon 11-8
Michael 16-45
Michaw 16-49
Michell 11-15
Mie Kin 11-21
Miers 17-21
Miligan 11-7
Millar 16-29
Miller 11-1,15,31,59,60;12-10,17;15-8;
    16-8,22,29,34,51;17-26
Millgan 15-18
Millikin 16-32
Mills 11-18;12-39
Minetes 11-16
Minis 16-11
Minnis 16-8,46
Mitchel 16-51
Mitchell 12-2,18,34;16-31,34,50,52;17-10
Mite 16-35
Mithas 12-8
Moan 12-10
Mochan 16-49
Moffat 15-19;16-51;17-24
Moffatt 17-10

Moffett 12-27
Moffit 11-14,44;12-2
Moffitt 12-1
Moiris 15-1
Molineauo 11-21
Mollan 11-62;16-40
Mollin 11-2
Molloghan 16-2
Mollony 11-16
Molloy 15-3
Mollyneux 12-7
Molone 12-12
Monaghan 12-32,39;16-17
Monahan 12-8
Monderson 16-45
Monegan 11-18
Money 16-42
Monk 17-10
Monogham 11-43
Montgomery 11-1,3,53;12-5,7;15-24;17-2
Moody 16-7
Moone 16-30
Mooney 11-60;16-23,35;17-21
Moony 17-11
Moor 12-29
Moore 11-1,14,31,51,58,59;12-2,3,13,1
    17,39;15-12,18,19,23,24;16-1,8,
    39,53;17-3,15,19,20
Moorhead 11-18,55
Moran 11-43;15-6
Morehead 17-24
Morehouse 17-18
Morer 16-40
Morgan 11-14,24;15-4;16-24
Morine 16-48
Morran 11-40
Morre 12-10
Morrin 7/25/12
Morris 12-13;16-20;17-6,10
Morrison 11-6,18;12-5;16-30,40;17-15,
Morron 11-4
Morrow 11-6,9,14;12-8;15-24;16-3,12
Morton 16-19
Mossop 17-19
Mubay 11-44
Mubrea 11-1
Muldary 16-39
Muldawney 15-6
Mulden 11-18
Mulhall 16-48
Mulhattan 12-32
Mulheris 12-10
Mulheron 16-51
Mulhollan 12-15
Mulholland 11-21;12-27;16-24,30

Mullan 12-11,27;15-8;16-10,12,28
Mullay 15-5
Mullen 16-36
Mulligan 16-2,45
Mullony 11-43
Mulvaney 16-36
Mulvany 15-6
Mulvenna 12-28
Mulvey 16-35
Munn 11-9
Murdoch 15-5;16-23
Murdock 11-25
Murdough 11-8
Murney 16-19
Murphy 10-1;11-5,14,19,20,24,44,58;
    12-3,4,7,27,39;15-1,12,24;16-6,
    13,14,18,20,28,36,37;17-8,11,13,
    18,21,26,28;7/20/16
Murray 11-47;12-19,31,33,34;15-17,23;
    16-4,13,17,27,39,40,52;17-14,
    17,27
Murrin 15-23
Murry 11-5,15,16,26;16-52
Murtagh 11-19;15-2;17-29
Murtaugh 16-48
M-u-any 17-9
Nailor 11-24
Nalty 16-15
Nanghten 16-47
Nanson 11-51
Narey 16-2
Nasby 11-6
Nasida 16-1
Neal 16-17
Nealis 11-60
Neall 10-1
Needham 11-24
Neelis 17-15
Neil 11-42,54;15-9
Neilson 11-6,15,38
Neill 16-49
Nein 12-8
Nelis 12-40
Nelson 11-15,17;17-15
Nesbit 16-33;17-24
Nevin 16-17
Newan 11-24
Newberry 16-11
Newlan 16-41
Newman 11-24
Nicholas 11-29
Nicholl 16-45
Nickle 15-16;16-28
Nickson 17-17
Nielson 11-3;16-31

Niven 16-47
Nixon 11-6
Nolan 16-15
Noone 16-30
Norris 11-18,51
Nowlan 16-41
Nowland 16-35
Nowlin 15-17
Nugent 12-3;15-10
Oats 12-2
O'Beirn 15-3
O'Boyle 16-24
O'Brien 10-1;11-5,25,43,47;12-19;
    15-19;16-15,39
O'Cain 16-30
O'Callaghan 8/3/16
O'Calloghan 8/3/16
O'Connell 15-6
O'Connor 16-39
O'Donnel 12-3;16-32,46;17-13
O'Donnell 11-55;12-8,34;15-4,18;
    16-24;17-7
Ogilby 16-37
O'Hara 13-1;16-5,41;17-11
O'Hare 16-22;17-9
O'Kean 12-10
O'Keef 12-3
O'Leary 15-14
O'Loone 16-30
O'Neal 11-15;16-17,37
O'Neall 16-31
O'Neil 15-5;16-10,30,32,33;17-29
O'Neill 11-7,55;12-7,13,18;16-3
O'Neils 12-10
O'Ray 11-14
O'Reilly 15-17;16-37;17-29
O'Rorke 11-60;15-3
Orr 11-6,35,38,58;12-15,29;16-11,42;
    17-9
Osborne 12-19;15-23
O'Shaughnessy 16-25
Owens 11-9
Owins 11-25
Pagin 17-29
Paine 11-21
Painter 15-9
Paisley 16-50
Palmer 16-31
Parcell 16-48
Park 11-3;12-30;16-25,28;17-23
Parker 11-4,5;12-15;16-10,23
Parks 11-60
Parr 16-40
Paschel 12-10
Patkinson 17-17

155

158

www.ingramcontent.com/pod-product-compliance
Lightning Source LLC
Chambersburg PA
CBHW050528270326
41926CB00015B/3117